Lose Weight
by Eating

THE SCANDINAVIAN DIET

Lose Weight by Eating

THE SCANDINAVIAN DIET

Published by Little Moon Publishing Ltd.,
3rd floor Premier House
12-13 Hatton Garden
London EC1N 8AN
UNITED KINGDOM
www.littlemoonpublishing.com

ISBN 978-1-908018-00-7

Text copyright Sten Sture Skaldeman © 2011
First English edition © 2011
Translated from Norwegian by Lisa Bostwick
Based upon the Swedish edition *"GI-Noll!"* and
Norwegian edition "GI-Null!"
Designed in Norway
Printed by Nørhaven in Denmark
Cover design by Kjetil Tørum, Norway

"This is an exceptionally intelligent and well-written book…Let's hope that the established nutrition experts open their eyes and realise that their recommendations are not as beneficial as what Skaldeman proposes."

Lidia Maria Berg, nutritionist
Marina de Paoli, PhD in Nutrition

"Lose Weight by Eating is so full of insightful observations that it should be required reading at all universities and colleges that teach courses in nutrition and health studies."

Dag Viljen Poleszynski, PhD in Nutrition
Editor, "VOF", (a Norwegian health magazine)

"I am a paediatrician. Sten Sture Skaldeman has done what children do – he has listened to his own body. He said no to carbohydrates when he realised they made him fat, and he said yes to fat when he realized that fat in his diet made him slim. Skaldeman has discovered that you don't turn green from vegetables, and you don't get fat from eating fat. Listening to your own body is a good principle to follow."

Bjørn Hammarskjöld, paediatrition,
PhD in Biochemistry

"I have used Skaldeman's principles for the past five years in my work as nutrition therapist. The results are unequivocal: More fat in the diet stimulates metabolism but also normalises the fat content in the blood (triglycerides). Changing to a high fat diet and limiting carbohydrate intake reinforces the immune system considerably, of which Skaldeman is a living example."

Jens Veierstad, nutrition therapist,
Arena Clinic, Oslo, Norway

About THE SCANDINAVIAN DIET and GI-Zero!

A revolution is happening in Scandinavia. Millions of people are rediscovering what they are designed to eat! In this book we use the term THE SCANDINAVIAN DIET to describe this natural way of eating.

It is a collective term which includes more specific diets. Sten Sture Skaldeman's weight loss program, GI-Zero!*, is one of them. This unique program will maximize your weight loss. It is easy, effective and healthy, and just like Skaldeman's thousands of successful followers, this program will benefit *you!*

If you have any questions or simply want to know more, please visit *www.thescandinaviandiet.com*

You can also check out these online resources:

> www.dietdoctor.com
> www.drbriffa.com
> www.livinlavidalowcarb.com
> www.marksdailyapple.com
> www.theharcombediet.com

* GI (Glycemic Index) is a measure of the effects of carbohydrates on blood sugar. GI-Zero! means zero increase in blood sugar and hence maximal weight loss. 'GI-diets' recommend food that raises your blood sugar levels slowly, the key to GI-ZERO!, on the other hand, is that it won't raise it at all!

Contents

A short preface

GI-Zero! Is my name for natural food that will stabilise your blood sugar levels and give you added health benefits too – one of them being radical weight loss.

A lot of what you will read here you won't find in other books. The explanation is simple: This is my own journey. I quickly discovered that accepted truths were not actually true.

Besides my own experience, GI-Zero! builds on what about 5000 women and men have told me about their own progress. Some of the women lost 8 stone (45 kg), while some men have lost 11 stone (70 kg). The large majority reduced their weight by half. No other weight plan can claim results like that.

Here is how you use the book: After reading the introductory section and the section about the three weight classes (8+, 4+ and 2+), choose the recipes and the procedures that suit your present body weight or your level of ambition.

Much of the book is recipes. While men are often satisfied with bacon and eggs, most women prefer more variation. You will find plenty of variety in these recipes. All of them are categorised and evaluated according to my dietary rules. I provide the calculations for carbohydrate and fat content for over 100 recipes.

I myself have lost 10 stone (65 kg) and regained my health. I am over 65 but am in better shape than when I was 30. Whether it's 1 stone or 8 (5 or 50 kg) you are looking to lose, you will find the recipes to accomplish it in this book.

Good luck to you!
Sten Sture Skaldeman

What should we be eating?

We should, of course, be eating what we were created to eat!

Humans are mammals, and we are governed by the laws of nature. We become healthy when we eat what we were created to eat, and we become sick when we eat unnatural food. Like other mammals, our bodies have mechanisms for natural weight regulation. But that weight regulation does not function if the way we eat conflicts with what is natural for us.

A gazelle grazing grass-rich plains never gets fat. The gazelle can eat from morning until night and still leap three times higher than a ballet dancer. A lion that watches food strolling by never gets fat. A lion also leaps three times higher than a ballet dancer – and does it with a gazelle between its teeth.

It is not possible to get fat on natural foods. All mammals have hormonally driven weight regulation that prevents excessive fat storage. Only humans, with their large brains, are dumb enough to make themselves sick by the way they eat. Other mammals eat the food that they were created to eat.

This entire book is about what you should eat to feel better in every way. You are going to eat real food, and you are not going to worry about fat or creamy sauces. In short, you are going to eat the food that your grandmother and grandfather ate. Visit your grandmother if she is still living and ask her for some cooking tips. She knows how to make healthy food, and she knows what butter and cream mean. If she has inherited a cookbook from her mother, ask to borrow it. You find the healthiest food in cookbooks that are a hundred years old!

If you are underweight, add lots of carbohydrates, for example, fruit, bread, and potatoes. Carbohydrates send fat storage signals and help you gain weight. If you are overweight, remove the carbohydrates and replace them with meat and fat. Fat sends fat-burning signals! This is the natural weight regulation that is one of the key principles in THE SCANDINAVIAN DIET.

Why do we eat like we do?

When we eat, it's not so much a matter of choice. In our everyday life, we eat what we are accustomed to eat, or what is put on the plate in front of us. If we don't like the food, we take small helpings. If we think it tastes good, we eat a lot. Some people eat – or don't eat – for moral reasons; others to please their mother-in-law or colleagues. Some people count calories and starve themselves regularly. When they are not starving themselves, they will often eat something just because it tastes good. Very few people eat to achieve the best possible health.

THE SCANDINAVIAN DIET is all about eating what is good for the body. This means that most of our food should come from happy animals that have lived natural lives. Supplement this with as many vegetables as possible. THE SCANDINAVIAN DIET prescribes vegetables that grow above ground, preferably organic vegetables you have grown yourself.

If we have the time and money, we should buy all our food from local producers. For most of us this is not possible. But every time we eat real food instead of industrially-produced food, we give the body a shot of vitamins. And every time we eat a product that some of our food manufacturers have messed with, it affects our vitality and immune system.

We should not pump diesel into a gas-driven car, and we should not put margarine in a human. These substances make the machinery freeze up. We should not eat bread made of nutrient-poor flour, and we should not eat hotdogs that primarily consist of water, chemicals, and scraps.

We should base our diet on natural foods. If we eat vegetables, they should be cultivated naturally, that is to say ecologically. We should be careful with fruit. The fruit that is in the grocery stores contributes to weight gain and loads the body with sugar and pesticides. Fruit sugar (fructose) affects the body similarily to regular cane sugar.

I started with the question: What should we eat?

The answer is that we should eat natural food. It's as simple as that.

But what does this mean in practice?

It means that we should base our diet on meat, fish, and poultry. Everything that moves is made to be eaten. We should supplement our diet with cheese, eggs, and butter. These are almost as good. For the extremely overweight, vegetables should be used as garnish. If you are mildly overweight, you can supplement your meals with salads and vegetable dishes that are low in carbohydrates. Bread should be avoided, and we must eat less fruit until weight loss is nearly achieved.

"Better a worm in the cabbage than no meat at all."
    Russian proverb

When should we eat?

I eat when I am hungry. If I am hungry in the morning, I eat in the morning. If I am not hungry until three o' clock, then I don't eat until three o' clock.

Don't be afraid! This isn't about you. Not yet! But it can be good for you to know what changes to expect. With THE SCANDINAVIAN DIET you will actually change your metabolism. You will teach your body to live on fat; giving yourself access to a new energy source – your own fat storeroom.

The nutritional "experts" say that we should eat breakfast. This is very true, but only if we are talking about carbohydrate eaters. Someone who uses sugar to fuel the body has to eat often. Otherwise, their blood sugar level drops dangerously low.

For those of us who eat natural foods, other rules apply. We are not at all dependent on having regular meals. We provide our body with food by way of our mouths when it wants food by way of our mouths. At other times, we get our nourishment from our reserves – the ones that we carry around our waists. The result is that we lose weight, because we burn fat and use it as energy

These ideas are probably new to you, but after a few months with THE SCANDINAVIAN DIET you will understand what I am talking about. When you have better access to your stored fat, you always have "food" available. A sugar eater eats only by mouth and stores the surplus as fat because the sugar turns off their fat metabolism.

When you eat natural food, you eat from your plate and also from your body's own reserves. This is why you are not hungry so often, and why you will soon be buying new trousers in smaller sizes!

You will probably be having less food on your plate when you eat GI-Zero! meals as part of THE SCANDINAVIAN DIET. This is due, in part, to the fact that the food you are now eating is more nutritious and also because you are taking some of your nourishment from your reserves. Thus, it is not important to constantly calculate the number of calories on your plate. The nutritional "experts" have yet to understand this, but this is one of the foundation blocks of a GI-Zero! way of life.

In short: we should eat when our bodies want food. People who eat for social reasons or just to have something to do, will continue being fat.

Eating your way to weight loss

LOSE WEIGHT BY EATING is a book about hormonally regulated weight control. It is not a book about starving or exercise.

With GI-Zero! we eat natural foods so that blood sugar levels stay stable with a minimal release of insulin. The goal is to release as little insulin as our ancestors did. When we have reached that goal, we stop storing unnecessary fat. At the same time we gain access to our fat reserves.

The point of GI-Zero! is that we always eat until we are satisfied, and that we never feel any "cravings". Stable blood sugar gives us protection and endurance. We eat when we need to eat, and if there is nothing to eat, we tap into our reserves. We function as humans are intended to function.

To understand the way our bodies regulate weight, we must look at our origins. We are descendants of prehistoric hunters who had carbohydrates available only a brief time each year. Those who were best at storing carbohydrates as fat had the greatest chance of surviving the long winter. The ability to store carbohydrates as fat was advantageous for a prehistoric hunter, but it is problematic in a society where people live on easily digested junk food.

Compare yourself to a brown bear. Bears store fat by way of carbohydrates (blueberries) and live on the fat all winter. If the bear were to eat a few moose instead of blueberries, it would starve to death while it hibernated. You can't get fat on moose!

People today don't need to store extra fat for winter. There-fore we should eat lots of moose and not so many blueberries. THE SCANDINAVIAN DIET will provide you the recipe.

"I can without problem eat whatever and as much as I want. The only thing that happens, is that I get fatter."
Unknown philosopher

Do we dare trust reality?

Reality can be thought of as a large-scale scientific study. Over the last thirty years we have been able to study what happens when people eat lots of bread, flour, sugar and artificially produced fat (margarine). Reality shows that these people become fat and sick.

We can all see the results of this thirty-year-long bread eating study out on the streets and in the shopping centres. Yet, the scientific establishment tells us that these results don't count, for they are not scientific enough. Observations that can be made by any and all are called "anecdotal experiences", says science.

I have lost over 10 stone (65 kg) by activating my body's natural weight regulation. This weight regulation is hormone driven, and you won't find anything about it in any nutritional textbooks. Therefore, many well-educated people think that this weight regulation simply doesn't exist!

Modern nutritional science maintains that human beings are the only mammals in the world who must starve themselves in order to lose weight. People who lose weight by eating only add to "anecdotal experience" and their stories are discounted by official "experts". Several thousand readers have written to me and shared such experiences.

So-called correct nutrition science is financed by the food industry and pharmaceutical firms. For some reason, nutrition science tells us that we should eat what is cheap to produce and lucrative to sell. When we eventually become ill from this food, the pharmaceutical firms have an arsenal of pills on hand.

With the help of pills we can lower blood pressure and cholesterol and force the body to release more insulin. If the body can't manage this, we can supplement the missing insulin. Insulin makes us fat, and it's not long before we need even more medicine. It is a great business concept. You make the choice to eat what is not good for your body and then take medicine to lessen the effects of the food. That is the scientific model.

Alternatively, you can do what I do and get healthy by eating natural foods. My model is called *GI-Zero!* which is a weight loss program using THE SCANDINAVIAN DIET.

"A doctor is an unfortunate person who each day is required to perform miracles i.e. to bring health into harmony with excess."
François Voltaire

Watch out for GI nonsense!

If you want to get rich selling dieting plans, you have to give your customers with what they want. You should preferably offer a brief diet program that lets them return to eating normal food quickly; the only difference to their old diet being that the label on the package now says "whole wheat".

"Follow my diet plan for a few weeks, and afterwards you can eat almost anything!" That is the short version of what most GI-gurus say.

Fruit is often permitted. Dark chocolate is permitted. Desserts with artificial sweeteners are permitted. It is a wonderful diet for someone who doesn't want to change their lifestyle. You can have your cake and eat it too!

The fact that this plan does not work over time is unimportant. Most of us lose a few stone in the beginning because the body loses water. We tell our friends about the fantastic GI-method. The easily marketed model acts like a chain letter, and before long the misguided low-carb expert has signed contracts with tabloids, TV-stations and businesses that produce food.

After a few weeks you can start to eat normally again, and then the weight loss stops. Your body retains water again, and your weight resumes its previous level. Indeed there are no magic "GI-foods" that can make you slim and healthy. Everyone who sells such plans and recipes does it out of self-interest.

Most of my students and readers have tried everything – and that apparently is necessary before they dare to try my radical concept. If you still don't feel convinced, the time is not yet right for you. You can always buy another misguided GI-book, one with wonderful desserts, or try yet another exercise program. When you know that you have tried everything, you are ready for GI-Zero! Then you are really ready to take hold of your life.

"There can never be enough healthy food, said the GI-expert, and sprinkled sugar on his honey!"

The "brilliant" plate plan

"The plate plan is a brilliant Swedish invention," says a Swedish weight loss professor. He refers to the idea that you lose weight by eating foods that stimulate fat storage. The only way to lose weight on such a diet is to eat small portions.

The professor is right about the plan being brilliant – brilliant, at least, for all those on the business side of the industry. The plate plan ensures that weight loss clubs (like Weight Watchers) have a permanent group of customers. It increases interest in the professor's weight club, and it creates long waiting lists with all the surgeons in the country who offer to remove part of the intestine.

The plate plan is an example of what is called "a balanced diet". It contains little fat, not very much protein, and an abundance of carbohydrates. It is actually very similar to the diet that sumo wrestlers use to achieve extreme weight gain. You can read more about how sumo wrestlers do this on page 191.

The basic mistake of the plate plan is that it is continually sending fat storage signals to the brain. This is what carbohydrates do. At the same time, the brakes are put on fat metabolism. Carbohydrates are responsible for this too. Anyone who wants to maintain their weight on such a diet must either limit their intake of food or get lots of exercise.

The plate plan does not originate in nutrition science, but in the agriculture politics. One of its central theories is that people get sick from the locally-produced food that they always have eaten. This food is expensive to produce and is replaced, in the plate plan, by margarine, bread and potatoes.

The plate plan message has been preached for over thirty years. It is originally based on the objectives of the American food industry. The practical consequences of this doctrine can be seen in today's USA. We are now starting to see it in other places as well – most notably Oceania, parts of the Middle-East, large parts of South America and, of course, the Western world.

What do calories mean?

If you eat according to THE SCANDINAVIAN DIET, you don't need to count calories. We eat to provide the body with the nutrients and the energy we need to function best. We eat to achieve the best possible health. How much energy the diet contains is irrelevant. But this applies only to those who eat in agreement with our hormonal principles. For those who eat in agreement with the officially recommended diet, completely other rules apply.

Most people who diet try to limit the number of calories they consume. They reduce their energy intake by eating less, or they increase their use of energy by exercise. They count calories in and calories out. I like to call it energy-driven dieting.

Energy-driven dieting works well in theory, but not so well in practice. People don't like to be hungry, and if they exercise enough they compensate for the exercise by eating more. Everyone who has tried this knows it to be true.

We who use THE SCANDINAVIAN DIET, eating along GI-Zero! principles, regulate our weight through the help of our built-in regulatory system. We don't starve our bodies, because that leaves us functioning at half speed. What we want is a body that functions optimally and produces benefits in the form of energy, love of life, and a strong immune system.

Eat less and run more, say the professors. If you gain weight, you are either eating too much or exercising too little. Other rules apply for those of us who eat according to GI-Zero! We eat so that we send fat metabolising signals to the body. This is natural weight regulation, and it has nothing to do with calories or exercise.

No mammal gets fat when it eats the food that it is created to eat. This also applies to the human mammal. There are many more calories in bacon than there are in sweet rolls, but no one has ever got fat by eating bacon.

Read more about calories on page 231.

Skaldeman's fat burning quotient is a better measurement

In this book, only two measurements are important. These are the amount of carbohydrates you consume – and "Skaldeman's fat burning quotient". I provide the amount of carbohydrates for all recipes in the book. My fat burning quotient is a measure that I use to make my days simpler, and it is also provided with each recipe.

Skaldeman's fat burning quotient is a flexible aid, intended for those who don't want to calculate forward or backward or use computer-based nutritional programs. You can use the fat burning quotient in the grocery store. All you have to do is read the list of ingredients on the package. You make a quick calculation and either buy the product or put it back on the shelf.

In my opinion, it is not enough that a product contains few carbohydrates. I would prefer that it contains a high proportion of fat as well. If not, the product is less healthy. Sounds crazy, but it's true!

Skaldeman's fat burning quotient is my invention, and it is a measurement that has become widely accepted by followers of THE SCANDINAVIAN DIET. It is based on the tenet that the fat in our food should weigh at least as much as the protein, and the carbohydrate portion should be low. It is even better, if the fat weighs twice as much as the protein.

What does this mean in practice? Well, if I eat 100 g of fat, 80 g of protein, and 20 g carbohydrate, the fat portion is equal to the sum of the other portions ($100 = 80 + 20$). The relationship is one to one.

Let's do this one more time: I eat 100 g of fat. I divide the weight of the fat by the weight of the remaining portions (80 g of protein and 20 g of carbohydrates). 100 divided by 100 is 1, so the fat burning quotient is 1.

Now that isn't so difficult, is it?

THE SCANDINAVIAN DIET is a program for health

One of the fundamental theses of this book is: "Eat as you were created to eat, and you will get the body and the health that you were created to have."

This is the basis of THE SCANDINAVIAN DIET. It is all about improved health, strength, and more satisfaction through eating. It is about sleeping better at night and waking up with new vitality.

If you are sick and overweight, you will eat your way to

weight loss and health. If you are afflicted with infections, sugar cravings, diabetes, infertility or have unexplained fatigue, your condition will improve or you may recover completely. GI-Zero! boosts the body's ability to heal itself. You can read more about the diet's effect on health later in this book.

The healing process happens in several steps. After about a week, your brain has adapted to the new diet, and you see the first result on the scales. After about a month, your body begins to understand what is going on, and it starts to metabolise fat seriously. After about a year, you are a new person, from the inside out. You have started to live a new life in a new body.

I dare claim that THE SCANDINAVIAN DIET even has an impact on your love life. You get a gleam in your eye on this diet. If you have a partner, he or she will become more attractive with each passing day!

The point of THE SCANDINAVIAN DIET is that it causes hormonal changes in the body. The hormonal change causes the body to use its fat reserves as energy, which is what you want first and foremost. But another equally important change is that you regain your zest for life. More joyful living in the broadest context will be yours, including enjoyment of food, exercise, and your partner.

GI-Zero! is perhaps primarily intended for women. Should you doubt my advice, try it on your husband. Put him on GI-Zero! When you see the results, it will become a team effort and you will have many pleasant years ahead of you!

Time to choose a program!

Welcome to your new life!

You have read the introductory sections and decided to practice THE SCANDINAVIAN DIET. It is a question of now or never, and now it's time to choose a specific program. You have three GI-Zero! groups to choose from: 8+, 4+ and 2+. Which group should you choose? If you weigh 16 stone (100 kg) too much, you belong in group 8+, and if your weight is close to normal, you should choose 2+. If you are one of those who have managed to keep a fairly normal weight, but gradually had to buy larger sizes over the course of several years, 4+ will probably be the best choice.

GI-Zero! is primarily a program for health. I had no idea that it would improve my health when I started this program with the goal of losing weight. Now I know that the health benefits are far greater and more important than the weight loss benefits. I myself have lost over 9 stone 6 (65 kg), but my health has improved much more than that.

It is extremely simple to eat your way to better health. This book provides you with the recipes. For most people, better health automatically leads to weight loss. A healthy body doesn't want to be fat!

GI-Zero! will give you a new life, but only when you follow the principles. If you gain weight easily, this is a radical change. Slimmer people with a few extra pounds around their waist can take an easier approach. Which group you belong to is your decision.

How to choose your group!

It is your sensitivity to carbohydrates that determines which GI-Zero! group functions best for you. Your actual weight is not as significant. The really important factor is your sensitivity to sugar, since all carbohydrates are eventually transformed to sugar in the body, just at different rates. Mashed potatoes make blood sugar levels rise faster than sugar, for example.

8+

Group 8+ is highly sensitive to carbohydrates. Obviously a tough approach is necessary to achieve good results. The prescription is animal fat. There is no other food that is as effective. As you will see in the recipes for this group, it is quite easy to make good food according to this program. The difference is that we eat meat, fish, butter and cream – and drop virtually everything else.

Three parts meat and one part fat is the most effective combination. You can eat fatty pieces of meat as they are. If the meat is lean, add some fat. The only addition is some green leaves for garnish. On exactly this program I lost 7 stone (45 kg) in nine months.

If you think that this program is a little too extreme, you can use the recipes for 4+. This is how I eat today, and with this program I have lost an additional 3 stone 2 (20 kg), but at a slower rate. It is advantageous to lose weight slowly over time.

4+

Group 4+ eats meat and fat as a basis, plus a modest amount of vegetables as side dishes. However, the only vegetables allowed are those that grow above the ground. High starch vegetables (root vegetables) and fruits must be avoided. And, of course, you must never touch bread and pasta. To lean meats you add fat. Most people achieve a significant weight reduction with these recipes. But the really overweight and difficult cases will achieve better results from group 8+.

The first step is to speed up fat metabolism. That is the primary goal. If you think that the 4+ program is too strict, choose the more "liberal" program for 2+. The results are less certain. The decisive factor is your sensitivity to insulin. If 2+ doesn't work for you, return to the 4+ program.

2+

Group 2+ has the largest flexibility. This is the group for those of you who weigh less than 2 stone (13 kg) too much, with perhaps a few extra pounds around the waist. You are probably not insulin resistant and can tolerate more protein and a lower amount of fat in your diet. Underweight people who want to normalise their weight should also select this group. You can add some extra fat to your diet, but often this is not necessary.

You may be only slightly overweight, but that doesn't mean that you will reach your desired weight more rapidly. It can take just as long for someone with normal weight to lose ten pounds as it takes for an extremely overweight person to lose five times as much. The explanation is that the body hangs on stubbornly to those last few extra pounds. Towards the end of a weight loss program, exercise can be effective. In the beginning, exercise doesn't have much of an effect. However, we should exercise if we can, because it is very good for our health!

When you have found the right group and are convinced that you can manage to follow the program, get started. Let's suppose that you have selected the program for 8+. Follow the program for three months and then evaluate your progress. If it's working for you, continue until you have at least halved the amount by which you are overweight. Then you can switch to the more "liberal" 4+ program. Or you can continue the 8+ program.

If you lose weight too rapidly on the 8+ program, you should switch to the 4+ program. Losing more than two pounds (1 kg) per week is not advantageous over a long period of time and will leave you with problems of surplus skin. Believe me! The same goes for people who start with the more "liberal" 4+ program. If you lose weight too quickly, change to the 2+ program.

If you maintain the same weight for over a month, do the opposite. Then you go from the 2+ to the 4+ or from the 4+ to the 8+. It is your sensitivity to carbohydrates that determines the appropriate program for you.

About the recipes

Some of the recipes work well for all the groups, and in some cases I provide a variation of the recipe for each group. For the most part, this means adding some carbohydrates for the more liberal groups. Other recipes contain a combination of nutrients and energy sources that work particularly well for the specific group.

I have, of course, taken into account the experiences of my many thousand students when I grouped the recipes. If a recipe is especially successful for moderately overweight people, I have written the recipe and placed it in the 2+ group even though it could have been placed in another group. A recipe that has been successful among students who weighed 24 stone (150 kg) ends up in the group 8+ for the same reason.

As a general rule, you can always select recipes from a more restrictive group. However, if you belong to a restrictive group, you should not, with very few exceptions, choose recipes from the more "liberal" groups. This is especially important for the old yo-yo dieters who have selected group 8+. They have, in principle, no flexibility and should take advantage of the renewed opportunities for the good life that THE SCANDINAVIAN DIET offers.

Skaldeman's fat burning quotient – revisited!

Fat divided by proteins and carbohydrates – that is Skaldeman's fat burning quotient. You read about my fat burning quotient earlier, but the term is so important that I must repeat it again here. I have used a lot of time to calculate proportions, now called the fat burning quotient, for all my recipes, and you must fully understand how it functions. Then you can quickly judge how beneficial or harmful food is.

Skaldeman's fat burning quotient is especially calculated for those of you who find it stressful to weigh and measure. When you consider buying food in the grocery store you can use the fat burning quotient. Your food should contain a lot of fat and only a few carbohydrates. If the fat weighs more than the rest, that is good. If, in addition, it contains few carbohydrates, you know that the food is healthy.

Skaldeman's fat burning quotient is the ratio between the fat and the other ingredients. The fat in the food should weigh at least as much as the sum of proteins and carbohydrates. Then the fat burning quotient is 1.0 or more. That is the number produced by dividing the fat by the sum of proteins and carbohydrates. If the fat weighs more, the fat burning quotient is higher than 1.0; if the fat weighs less than the rest, the fat burning quotient is lower. With THE SCANDINAVIAN DIET we are looking for a high fat burning quotient.

Let's take a look at a hamburger (without the bread), for example. It has a fat burning quotient of 0.75. We arrive at that number by dividing the weight of the fat by the weight of the protein. The carbohydrates in this case are zero, but be aware that many hamburgers contain some grams of carbs. A 100 g hamburger contains 15 g fat and 20 g protein. 15/20 = 0.75. Therefore, the hamburger has a fat burning quotient 0.75. If you want a higher fat burning quotient, you can add a fatty cream sauce.

A fat burning quotient of 0.75 is often sufficient in group 2+, but in group 8+ we aim for a higher value.

The fat burning quotient for some minced meat types:

– Beef mince, 100 g (3.5 oz). 15/20. Fat burning quotient: 0.75.
– Beef mince supplemented with a fifth portion of cream. Fat burning quotient : 1.1.
– Pork and beef mince, 50/50. Fat burning quotient: 1.0.
– Pork mince, 20/16. Fat burning quotient: 1.25.

It is easy to understand the principle. The fattier the product is, the higher the fat burning quotient is. Skaldeman's fat burning quotient is a simple tool that I use to avoid weighing and measuring. In the beginning, you can read the list of ingredients in the product, but after a short time you know the contents of different food products. A requirement for the fat burning quotient to work is that the carbohydrate content is kept low.

I don't weigh food anymore. I know approximately what a portion weighs, and that is good enough for me. Now it is sufficient for me to eat a high proportion of animal products. When I go to the grocery store, I look for meat of all kinds and primarily select the fattier cuts. For obvious reasons, it is easier to find fatty bacon than fatty tenderloin. Fatty cuts of meat always have a high fat burning quotient.

Whole cuts with much of the fat intact are best, but they

are sometimes difficult to find. For me, a bison hump would be the very best thing, but where can I find that?

I solve this problem in two ways:

- When the family eats meat, I work as the "rubbish bin" and take all the fatty pieces. Rib-eye steak and pork chops retain a lot of their fat. Pork is sometimes lean, but if the fat isn't removed, it contains a substantial amount!
- Alternatively I use minced meats. Two parts minced pork and one part beef mince form the basis for my dieter's meatballs. (Note that shop-bought minced meat mixtures are not as good because they often contain too little fat).

If I don't have food of this kind available, I eat something that is lean and supplement it with fat. Lean fried pork with butter works well. I use a tablespoon of butter per 100 g (3.5 oz) pork tenderoin. It is best with unsalted butter and lightly salted pork tenderloin. I have a positive attitude toward salt, but it binds fluids and makes it more difficult for those who want to measure their progress on the bathroom scales.

Minute steak* is actually lean, but if you fill it with cheese and add some extra butter, it contains enough fat. The principle is simple. The leaner the meat is, the more fat you should add. This is particularly important for the 8+ group. You can eat sizeable portions if you distribute your food intake over several large meals. Eating between meals should be avoided. If you eat too much, weight loss stops because the body survives on the food that you are consuming (the fat that you eat). If you eat too little, weight loss eventually reaches a standstill. The trick is to find a balance between eating until you are satisfied yet are still losing weight.

* A steak, similar to a large, thin hamburger, made from mince or ten-derised beef.

I suggest that you abandon complicated calculations. Calculating energy percentage is a whole science in itself. Control the carbohydrate content and use my fat burning quotient. If you use my recipes, these values are already provided.

When mother-in-law comes for a visit!

I will conclude this introduction with a little dieting psychology. I have halved my body weight. An important explanation for how I managed to do this, is that I stopped being "nice". I stopped eating like other people wanted me to eat. This sounds simple, but in reality it isn't.

People who live on desert islands have no problem maintaining a strict line. The rest of us will always be exposed to temptations or forced to eat something that is not part of our new program. It may be lunch with your colleagues at work, a conference at a hotel, or a piece of birthday cake at a birthday party.

"A little piece of cake can't make a difference," says your hostess. "You have lost so much weight …"

We are polite, eat what we shouldn't eat, and keep rolling along. Many who write to me tell about how a piece of cake at work turned into a formidable catastrophe. It is not the single piece of cake – that means nothing. It is the body and the brain's reaction to the piece of cake that means something.

Let us say that you belong in the 8+ group. In that group it is forbidden to be "nice". From now on you have to think like this: "I am losing half of my excess weight. Nothing else is as important. I am not going to budge an inch until I lose half of my excess weight. No matter what! When I have 4 stone left to lose I will have more options. Until I reach that point I am going to stay on course and continue to burn fat." And you can think the same way if you start dieting in group 4+ or 2+.

But still your mother-in-law comes to visit! You probably feel like you should make an exception, to keep harmony in the house, but you don't want to give in to the sugar temptation again. What do you do?

There is really no problem here, you can make as many exceptions as you want – as long as they are only for your mother-in-law. Give her pudding if you want to. Bake cakes and sweet rolls. Meanwhile, you should eat a spinach frittata or some of my other recommended side dishes!

Consider, too, that it is not necessary to eat biscuits with your tea or coffee. There is no natural law that commands biscuits, cookies, cupcakes, doughnut or any other sweet treat. It may seem a little insulting to eat something different than your guests. You can offer them a delicious sandwich with lots of sliced meat instead – something that is an approved part of your diet. Your mother-in-law doesn't need to know that the "bread" is carbohydrate-free. Or you can make a few sandwiches for yourself that look the same on the surface. Another good alternative is to make the wonderful *smörgåstorta*, a classic Swedish open salty cake-like sandwich, that is the last recipe for the 8+ group.

In a crisis, you can always "borrow" a recipe from a more liberal group. If you belong to the 8+ group, a shrimp sandwich in the 4+ group is not too much of a problem. If you are extra careful, you can serve your mother-in-law a normal shrimp sandwich – I guarantee that she won't notice any difference between your plate and hers.

Those who belong in the 8+ group can't afford more excess than this. No deviations are allowed in the 4+ group either, but when you reach that group you have at least lost 4 stone (25 kg). Then you will want to maintain your weight loss. It is the journey from the 8+ to the 4+ group that is the most risky. A little bump in the road can tip the cart. When you have reached the 4+ group, you are on a paved road.

The same reasoning can be used for other groups. If you start in the 4+ group, make a solid commitment to achieve half of your weight loss without any deviation. Then you only have a few pounds left before you are in the 2+ group. This will inspire you. When you finally reach the 2+ group you have reached a result that is worth maintaining. Thus the road stretches open before you.

Those of you who start in group 2+ have more freedom. Nine grams of carbohydrates per meal gives you some flexibility. If you save the carbohydrates in the course of the day, you can allow yourself some tasty side dishes at dinner. But stick to my list of carbohydrates. Bread, pasta, and potatoes don't belong in any part of THE SCANDINAVIAN DIET.

A quick introduction to healthy cooking

How do you make food with few carbohydrates? How do you manage to eat enough useful fat? What should you eat for breakfast? How do you make herb butter, sauces, and dressings that are appropriate for GI-Zero? In this introductory chapter intended for all the groups, 8+, 4+ and 2+, you will get answers to questions like these.

If you want to prepare food in another way, you are free to do so. What follows here is the food that my students and I make and eat to lose weight.

Following this introductory cooking course there are three groups of recipes. The strict recipes in the 8+ group are intended for very overweight people who have tried everything. Now they will finally get a program that works. Group 4+ has more flexibility, but even these recipes are stricter than most you encounter in other programs (the ones that look great but don't work). When you finally reach the 2+ group, life gets simpler.

I still eat according to group 4+, even though I stopped losing weight several years ago. This is the food that suits my body. Sometimes I break my own rules with gusto. When you have finished your weight loss process, you can indulge yourself occasionally. Don't do this, however, until you have lost weight, or you will ruin several months of work in the course of a week!

Starting the day

Following the GI-Zero! program for dinner is simple. Most people manage that. Lunch is a little more difficult, especially if you eat out. It is best to take a packed lunch from home. What causes the most difficulty in the beginning is the first meal of the day.

Most people who read this book want to eat breakfast, and they should do so. Breakfast is a pleasant way to start the day, along with a cup of coffee and the morning paper. But what should we eat when we are following the GI-Zero! program? Female students often say that they want to avoid cooking in the morning, and that they want to have some variation in their diet.

People who would like some variation in their diet have often eaten low-fat yoghurt or cereal every day for the past ten years or more. For some reason or another, this hasn't seemed repetitive to them. But when they start eating a natural diet, they react negatively. This is an interesting phenomenon. The obstacle is probably not that the natural diet is monotonous, but that these individuals are not sufficiently motivated to change their diet.

So you have to find something that you can eat in the morning, something you enjoy, and something that is easy to vary. Why not start the day with a salad? You will arrive at bacon and eggs soon enough. A satisfying salad can be prepared in the time it takes to boil an egg. And a salad is much better and more natural than low-fat yoghurt and cereal.

Tuna fish salad

I think that a quick tuna fish salad is great. This is what I do:

1. Mix some chopped onion, Dijon mustard and lemon juice in a bowl.

2. Add some tinned tuna and a good dollop of mayonnaise.

3. Mix with a fork for 30 seconds, and the salad is ready!

If you want to add some spices, you can, but it really isn't necessary. On rare occasions, I might add some dill. The salad can be eaten as it is, or a hardboiled egg can be added.

Without the egg the salad contains 370 kcal and 3 g carbohydrates. The fat burning quotient is 1.45. I have calculated the use of half a tin of tuna fish in oil. Tuna fish in water has a catastrophically low fat burning quotient. If you add an egg the salad has 3.6 g carbohydrates, and with a handful of lettuce you come up to 4.7 g. But the fat burning quotient is still a good 1.24.

Quick tuna fish omelette

If you would rather eat your tuna fish warm, it can be done just as quickly. Fry the tuna fish quickly in a pan with butter, and mix in a few egg yolks. Season to taste and eat with a dollop of mayonnaise.

Half a tin of tuna fish, 1 tbs butter, 2 egg yolks and 1 tbs mayonnaise contains 600 kcal and 0.2 g carbohydrates. Fat burning quotient: 2.3.

Mackerel with onion and egg

We should eat mackerel at least once a week. Previously, I always had a stack of tins of mackerel in tomato sauce standing in my cupboard. It is inexpensive and good food. Mackerel in tomato sauce (beware – it contains sugar!) has some carbohydrates, but to all intents and purposes pepper mackerel or smoked mackerel contains no carbohydrates.

I mix a tin of mackerel with half a chopped onion and some drops of lemon juice. I eat this with a hardboiled egg. In the beginning, I used to spread it on a slice of sourdough rye bread. That was when I still had trouble losing weight.

When I cut out the bread, I started losing weight. It is tragic, because I really like sourdough rye bread.

A tin of mackerel with onion, lemon juice and two hard-boiled eggs contains 350 kcal and 4.6 g carbohydrates. Fat burning quotient: 0.7. If I had it on a slice of bread (90 g) it would come up to 600 calories, 48 (!) g carbohydrates, and a fat burning quotient of 0.34. Even though these 48 carbohydrates metabolise slowly, it doesn't help because they are transformed into sugar! They make your blood sugar levels rise and your body secrete insulin – and insulin prevents the metabolism of fat!

Fast shrimp and avocado salad

You always have an avocado in the house. You always have shrimp in the freezer and mayonnaise in the refrigerator. You have lemons and you have hardboiled eggs. What are you waiting for?

I ate incredible amounts of shrimp when I was losing weight. Not so much in the morning, then it was bacon and eggs, but later in the day I ate shrimp in combination with other food. The most important of which was mayonnaise!

Shrimp is a lean meat and mayonnaise is necessary to reach a good fat burning quotient.

To make this salad:
1. Put half an avocado and a sliced hardboiled egg on a plate.
2. Top with about a cup of thawed shrimp (remove from the freezer a day before).
3. Sprinkle with lemon juice.
4. Add a dollop of mayonnaise.
5. Garnish with some dill.

I can put this salad together in less than a minute. But I cheat with the egg. I cut it in the centre and eat it with a spoon. It doesn't look as attractive, but everything gets mixed up in my stomach anyway. If it takes you more than a minute to make this salad, you must have very slow motor skills.

A cup of shrimp contains approximately 78 calories, less than 1 g carbohydrates, and has a fat burning quotient of almost zero. With a glob of mayonnaise you can reach a fat burning quotient of almost 1. Those of you who are very overweight will lose weight more rapidly if you eat shrimp with mayonnaise instead of shrimp without mayonnaise. This is due to the fact that mayonnaise stimulates the metabolism of fat; also, the meal keeps you satisfied longer so that you don't need to eat between meals. Snacking is not conducive to weight loss!

The only problem with mayonnaise is that is made from plant fats and animal fats are better for you. You can improve the balance by mixing the mayonnaise with crème fraîche.

The fat burning quotient for these simple salad components are:

- Shrimp, fat burning quotient 0.06
- Egg, fat burning quotient 0.76
- 200 g (7 oz) shrimp, 1 tbs mayonnaise, fat burning quotient 1.0
- 200 g (7 oz) shrimp, 1 egg, 1 tbs mayonnaise, fat burning quotient 0.95
- 200 g (7 oz) shrimp, 1 egg, 1/2 avocado, 1 tbs mayonnaise, 1 tsp. lemon juice, fat burning quotient 1.1

The salad with avocado, egg, shrimp, and mayonnaise has 422 calories and 4.4 carbohydrates. But a fat burning quotient of 1.1 is an excellent breakfast. If you add 1 tbs crème fraîche then you get a portion of useful saturated fat. This salad totals 490 calories and 5 g carbohydrates. Fat burning quotient: 1.3.

Even quicker shrimp salad

If you want a quick start to the day, put frozen shrimp in the refrigerator the day before. And, of course, you have hard-boiled eggs in the refrigerator. You should always have some hardboiled eggs on hand.

It may seem unnecessary to offer a recipe for this salad, but then there are people who write to me and ask how to boil an egg!

To make a quick and simple salad:
1. Put a few lettuce leaves on a plate. Spread slices of a hard-boiled egg on the edge along with the shrimp.
2. Add mayonnaise.
3. Garnish with lemon wedges and some dill.

This quick and easy breakfast provides between 400 and 500 kcal. It contains about 3 g of carbohydrates and the fat burning quotient is 0.6.

The quickest omelette

1. Melt butter in frying pan.
2. Add an egg and 2 egg yolks.
3. Add 1 tbs cream.
4. Mix, gather, and turn with spatula.
5. Your omelette is ready!

I season with lemon pepper and eat it with something warm or cold. This quick omelette goes with everything!

The omelette alone provides 340 kcal, 1.5 g carbohydrates and a fat burning quotient of 1.9. A tin of mackerel in tomato sauce adds extra carbohydrates. Scrape off the tomato sauce! A breakfast like this provides 500 kcal and has a fat burning quotient of 1.3. Mackerel is a real vitamin bomb. It covers 100% of your daily need for the critical vitamin D and 500% of vitamin B_{12}, which vegetarians often lack. Compare this with eating two pounds (1 kg) of cooked broccoli. Then you get 0% vitamin B_{12} and 0% vitamin D, and broccoli is one of our healthiest vegetables …

The omelette goes well with fried smoked ham that you can prepare at the same time. With 100 g (3.5 oz) of ham the calories amount to the same as with mackerel, but the fat burning quotient drops to 1.0. Ham is a lean meat.

Bacon and eggs

I ate bacon and eggs almost every day while I was losing weight. For breakfast or lunch. Sometimes I added ham or a pork chop, but most often it was regular bacon. The salt didn't bother me then.

When my wife makes breakfast it is often bacon and fried eggs; however, I really enjoy a bacon omelette or bacon and scrambled eggs. Omelette and scrambled eggs take the same amount of time when I stand at the stove.

How I make a bacon omelette:

I fry the bacon at medium heat. When it is almost done, I add an egg, a few egg yolks, plus 1 tbs cream. I turn down the heat and mix occasionally while the omelette stiffens.

If you make the omelette with three rashers of bacon, it provides about 500 calories and 1.5 g carbohydrates. Fat burning quotient: 1.7.

Sometimes I want scrambled eggs. Then I fry the ham or bacon in a pan while I fix the eggs in another pan. Or I eat the scrambled eggs with a piece of smoked fish or something else. Cold meatballs with feta cheese taste great with scrambled eggs.

100 g feta cheese and some scrambled eggs provide 600 kcal and 2.4 g carbohydrates. Fat burning quotient: 1.35.

Scrambled eggs

It is easy to make scrambled eggs.

1. Put a thick-bottomed frying pan on the stove. Melt a dollop of butter over low heat.
2. Break as many eggs as needed into a bowl. Add salt and
   pepper and a dash of cream. Mix well and pour into the
   pan.
3. Turn with a spatula until the eggs reach the desired consistency. I add some coarse pepper at the end.

A little scrambled egg made with 1 tbs butter, 2 eggs, and 1
tbs cream provides 350 kcal and 1.6 g carbohydrates. Fat
burning quotient: 2.0.

The easiest breakfast of all

Today, the breakfast I usually eat consists of leftovers from
dinner the day before. For those of you who would like to
avoid making food in the morning, this is a great alternative.
If you have just abandoned the nutrient-poor breakfast con-
sisting of yoghurt, cereals and whole wheat bread, this can
be a big step to take. In half a year you will look at this a
little differently.

It isn't necessary to push yourself, because your body will
steer the process. When you eat more nutrient-rich foods,
all your taste preferences will change. You gradually start to
eat like humans were intended to eat, and today's over-
sugared and over-salted foods lose their attraction.

Let this change happen naturally. In half a year you have
put the sugar urge behind you. Then you can live life fully.

Sauces, salad dressings, and herbed butters

Now we will address something pleasant, the good sauces and tasty butter that you should add to fried meats. The wonderful thing about THE SCANDINAVIAN DIET is that we don't need to be afraid of fatty side dishes and sauces.

This doesn't mean that we should drown food in fat, for most fat occurs naturally in good, well-marbled meat. Neither are we going to pour ⅓ litre cream over everything, like one of my students did, but we are going to enjoy good sauces and herbed butters.

I fry a lot of my food, so making a sauce is never a problem. Sometimes I just add something to the frying pan when the meat is browned. Put a lid on, and let it boil down. If the taste is too strong, I add some cream or boiling water. I serve the meat and the sauce together. It can't get any simpler. Just remember that the sauces must not be made with flour!

This is what you do:

Add water, bouillon, or wine to the pan and boil it down. When everything has dissolved, add some cream and simmer. A bit of butter towards the end makes a sauce smooth and shiny.

Usually the seasonings already in the pan are sufficient. If you want more taste you can add some soy sauce, Dijon mustard, anchovy brine, capers, lemon or something else that you like. If you want a sauce with a stroganoff flair, use onion, sugar-free tomato purée and lemon juice. If you want something in the direction of a béarnaise sauce, you need vinegar, onions, and tarragon. The options are endless – use your imagination!

Some more labour-intensive sauces

Cold sauces are primarily based on mayonnaise. Seasoning determines the kind of sauce. As you probably know, mayonnaise consists of egg yolks, oil, and either vinegar or lemon juice. It is simple to make mayonnaise yourself, but it is even easier to buy mayonnaise and mix in other ingredients. In this chapter, I present some recipes.

Warm sauces like béarnaise and hollandaise build on comparable principles, but here we use butter instead of oil. And often we prepare the sauce in a double boiler. Some simple recipes are presented for these as well.

You can make really advanced sauces with the help of an old cookbook – but the difference in taste is minimal, and I don't think they warrant the amount of extra work.

If you're in a hurry, you can always put some knobs of butter on your meat. I often do this when I eat steak rare. The butter melts together with some seasoning and crushed garlic. On a piece of well-matured meat, butter can be just as good as a carefully prepared béarnaise sauce.

You need only two sauces to accompany fried meats and only one for boiled meats. These sauces can be varied in an infinite number of ways, and flour is unnecessary. Other recipes for sauces are included as well, but we will start with these main sauces. (Just don't forget that sauces contain carbohydrates, even without flour! To be certain I usually calculate 2 g carbohydrates per 500 ml (just under a pint) of sauce.)

Sauce for fried and grilled meats

When the meat is browned, add a little cream and crème fraîche, and let the mixture boil down. If the meat is well seasoned, this will be enough. I usually season meats lightly, so I often add some crumbled feta cheese and 1 tsp Dijon mustard. Cover the frying pan and let the sauce simmer. The result is a perfect sauce, and everything is in one pan! If I have added too much feta cheese or Dijon mustard, I just add a little more cream. Sometimes I also add lemon juice.

You can also put the meat on a hot plate or in the oven, add a little white wine and cream to the frying pan, and let the mixture boil down while stirring constantly. Pour the sauce over the meat. (This method is perfect for pepper steak. I season the meat properly with coarsely ground pepper and allow it to rest for an hour before I fry it.)

Sauce for fried fish

I prefer cold sauce on fried fish, and it only takes a couple of minutes to make. I pour about 100 g (3.5 fl oz) of crème fraîche in a bowl, add a dollop of mayonnaise and 1 tsp Dijon mustard.

Afterwards, I add freshly squeezed lemon juice to taste. Perhaps a little cayenne pepper too. The sauce is ready! (If I want some colour to the sauce, I add some ground bell pepper or some sugar-free tomato purée.)

You don't need any other sauces for most fried meats, and flour isn't necessary to make a good roué.

Sauces for boiled meats

Suppose that you have boiled a chicken or some lamb. When the meat is almost done, remove some of the broth and let it boil down in a large pot. When you have the taste you like, add some cream, lemon juice, and seasonings. Curry is good with chicken, dill and lemon juice are good with lamb.

You must never thicken your sauces with flour, potato starch, corn starch, arrowroot, or anything similar. If you want a thicker sauce, add an egg yolk. That is the classic recipe. An egg yolk is equivalent to a few teaspoons of flour and tastes better. Just remember to stir constantly and keep the heat moderate. The sauce should just barely simmer. If you let sauces containing egg yolks boil or fail to stir them constantly, you will get lumps in the sauce.

Mayonnaise

The basis for cold sauces is mayonnaise or perhaps crème fraîche. It is simple to make a classic mayonnaise. There are three basic rules to follow:

1. Make sure the ingredients have the same temperature.
2. Add oil slowly in the beginning.
3. Mix thoroughly.

Ingredients:
- 2 egg yolks
- 1–2 tsp white wine vinegar or lemon juice
- 1 tsp Dijon mustard
- 30 ml neutral oil, not virgin olive oil!
- Salt and pepper

Instructions:
1. Put the egg yolks in a heavy bowl. Set the bowl on a wet towel so that it doesn't slip.
2. Mix in the mustard and half of the vinegar. Add seasoning.
3. Put the oil in something that allows you to pour carefully. Now you are ready to start. In a minute or two your mayonnaise is finished !

4. Mix rapidly as you slowly add the oil drop by drop. When the sauce starts to thicken, start trickling the oil a little faster. Don't try to hurry, and make sure that the oil is blending into the mayonnaise.

5. If the mayonnaise is too thick, add some lemon juice or cold water. If it separates, mix rapidly while you add a little boiling water. Many people choose to end the process with a few tbs boiling water, just to get the desired consistency. (If you can't get the separated sauce to combine, make a new base of egg yolks and vinegar and add it gradually into the separated mayonnaise.)

Flavoured mayonnaise

Here you are free to choose. You can add almost anything to mayonnaise. Many of the seasonings used give their name to the sauce. Mixing mayonnaise with crème fraîche or sour cream is often a good start.

Dill mayonnaise

Dill mayonnaise is a classic sauce for cold salmon. I usually mix two parts mayonnaise to one part sour cream and season to taste. Lemon juice is necessary; one or two tbs anchovy brine is good too. Sometimes I add a little Dijon mustard. The dill should be fresh and attractive, and be added last.

Remoulade sauce

- 20 ml mayonnaise
- 1 tbs minced gherkins
- 1 tbs chopped capers
- 1 tbs chopped parsley

This is a sauce that suits most seafood, but remoulade contains carbohydrates so eat it in moderation.

Green mayonnaise

- 20 ml mayonnaise
- 1 tbs blanched, finely chopped spinach
- 1 tbs chopped herbs, for example tarragon or chervil
- 1 tbs chopped parsley

Excellent for all cold fish dishes.

Warm butter sauces

Béarnaise and hollandaise are warm sauces made with butter. It is almost impossible to ruin them. Butter sauces are made just like you make mayonnaise, with butter instead of oil. Otherwise the principle is just as simple. You use egg yolks and something sour, and mix it with the fat. Heat is used to help the combination. If the sauce starts to separate, add a cold liquid. That is all that you need to know.

My béarnaise

I have some half-melted butter ready, and a few egg yolks in a glass. Then I am ready to start.

1. I boil up a sauce base from a few tbs minced onion, 100 ml white wine, and a few tbs white wine vinegar. Salt and pepper. And some tarragon of course! Without tarragon, no béarnaise! The sauce base boils down until there are only a few tbs left. Perfectionists strain the mixture and use only the liquid, but I don't.
2. I put the saucepan to the side, let it cool, and fold in a few egg yolks. Usually it gets thick quickly.
3. I put the saucepan back on the stove and start to carefully mix in the butter. Slowly in the beginning, with strong beating movements after a while. The sauce usually gets thick and smooth without any trouble.

4. The next step should be done in a double boiler, but I have had success doing it right on the burner. The trick is to turn the heat on for brief periods of time and then turn it off. The sauce shouldn't boil, just simmer gently.
5. If the sauce starts to clump, add more liquid. This can be vinegar, lemon juice, white wine, or a little cold water.

People say that it is difficult to make warm butter sauces, but I have never had a problem. If the sauce separates, which has never happened to me, the cookbooks say that you should mix a few egg yolks in another saucepan and fold them into the separated sauce, beat gently at first and then stronger as the sauce starts to combine.

Nic's Hollandaise

The simplest butter sauce is made by mixing all the ingredients in a pan and then warming everything at once while beating strongly. That is the principle behind Nic's Hollandaise.

Instructions:

1. Put 100 g (3.5 oz) cold butter into a saucepan.
2. Add 3 egg yolks, 2 tbs lemon juice, and a dash of thyme.
3. Let this stand for one hour.
4. When the meat is ready, put the saucepan on the stove and bring to a boil while stirring constantly. Using a double boiler will help you avoid the sauce sticking to the bottom of the pan.
5. Add lemon juice and pepper to taste.

Classic cream sauce

1. Bring about 200 ml (7 fl oz) of cream to the boil.
2. Mix an egg yolk.

3. Fold the egg mixture into the boiling cream. Turn down the heat and stir until thick.

4. Add salt and pepper to taste (some people use a little sugar, but we skip that).

Several simple sauces

You can cover all occasions with the above sauces. If you would like some variation, old cookbooks have much to offer. You can also find many recipes on the internet. Here are a few examples, my own and others. Start by making a classic stock.

Stock is healthy

Are your joints sore? Eat more broth! Stock is healthy, and it is perfect in all kinds of cooking. Today we make too little stock; in the past, cooks always had something boiling on the stove.

You can buy inexpensive meats and make excellent stock. Ask for bones for your dog! I keep the stock when I boil large portions of meat and let it continue to simmer at low heat. Sometimes I let it simmer overnight. I add some root vegetables (carrots, potatoes, swede), but I strain them off at the end.

I reduce the stock until it is quite concentrated. Then I freeze it in small portions, like in self-closing ice cube bags. Strain the stock into an ice cube bag, turn it upside down and it closes itself. When you need bouillon, you press out as many cubes as you need. Then you can make a perfect sauce in no time. Defrost, add cream, and reduce.

Classic shrimp sauce, classic soup

A fond is a concentrated stock. Here is a recipe for a superb fond. With this fond as a base, you can make the most fantastic shrimp sauce or shrimp soup if you prefer. The best thing about it is that you use only the shrimp shells. You can eat the shrimp themselves with mayonnaise, egg, and asparagus, or you can put them in a soup.

I usually make a large portion when I am first underway. This fond is perfect to have in the freezer:

Ingredients:
- 1 kg (2 lb 3 oz) fresh shrimps with shells
- 2 yellow onions
- A dash of olive oil
- A little sugar-free tomato purée
- 1 l (1.75 pints) fish stock

For the soup you need:
- Cream
- Seasoning to taste

Instructions:
Peel the shrimps and sauté the shells in olive oil. I use the head, legs, and caviar – everything except the shrimp. Don't worry about the smell!

When the shrimp shells have lightened in colour, add the finely chopped onion and the tomato purée (about ½ a tablespoon) and then add the fish stock. The job is almost done. Classic food is simple and easy to prepare.

When the mixture has simmered for twenty minutes, you have the beginning of a great fond. Using this fond you can enter into competition with any master chef. Drain off the liquid and enjoy the result. The stock can be frozen as it is, or reduced further to a finished fond. It's up to you.

If you are making a soup or a sauce:

1. Start to reduce the shrimp stock. Take your time. Reduce to less than half the liquid.
2. When the fond is ready, add cream and let the sauce simmer for 15 minutes. Add more cream to achieve the desired consistency. I add salt, pepper, and cayenne pepper to taste. Maybe a little lemon juice.
3. If the sauce is going to be a soup, I add the shrimp just prior to serving. They have to be warm – but if they boil, they get tough.
4. If you want to thicken the sauce, use egg yolks, not flour. Take the soup off the burner and stir in an egg yolk or two. Mix well. Then slowly bring the soup almost to a boil. If you let it boil, clumps will form.

The soup can be eaten as soup; the sauce can be used in the ground pike recipe on page 109. Calculate about 1 g carbohydrate per 10 ml of sauce. As a sauce, the fat burning quotient is 5; as a soup it is 1.0. This is due to the shrimp in the soup. The protein lowers the fat burning quotient.

Blue cheese sauce

Cheese sauce tastes good with most foods. I prefer to use a delicious blue cheese. I don't use a recipe; I just sauté a little green onion, add crème fraîche and a dash of inexpensive white wine. I add half a cube of chicken bouillon too. And sometimes cream. Use what you have available. Finally, I crumble a good piece of blue cheese into the mixture and simmer.

I add seasonings to taste, but usually further seasonings are unnecessary. Instead I often add more cream. The carbohydrate total depends on what you put in it. Calculate half a gram per tablespoon.

Super simple cheese sauce

Carefully heat some cream and crumble a tasty cheese into the cream. Parmesan is perfect, also gorgonzola. When the cheese has melted, the sauce is ready! I can eat a sauce like this on almost anything.

Malba's cold sauce

This easy sauce is an excellent sauce for Fakir steak (see page 91), grilled meats, or as a mild dip.

Instructions:
1. Put 200 g (7 oz) crème fraîche in a bowl.
2. Chop 5–6 sun-dried tomatoes in oil. Try to choose a brand with few carbohydrates. Mix into crème fraîche.
3. Season with garlic to taste.
4. Season with salt and pepper if you think it necessary.

My mild shrimp sauce

1. Sauté about 100 g (3.5 oz) shrimp in butter. A few minutes is sufficient.
2. Remove the shrimp from the pan. Deglaze with cream.
3. Simmer at low heat.
4. Season to taste. Tarragon is recommended. A dash of cognac also tastes good.
5. Add the shrimp and round off the sauce with some butter.

If you would like a stronger taste, use fresh shrimp shells. This makes a perfect sauce for fish pâté. Recipes for such sauces abound in old cookbooks.

Rhode Island sauce

Here we have a classic sauce. The chilli sauce contains quite a few carbohydrates, so use it with moderation.

Ingredients:
- 10 ml mayonnaise
- 5–10 ml chilli sauce
- 10 ml cream
- Cayenne pepper or Tabasco sauce

Mix the mayonnaise and the chilli sauce. If you carefully fold in whipped cream, you will have a lovely, light sauce. Heighten the taste with Tabasco or cayenne pepper. A dash of salt if you think it necessary.

With equal parts cream, chilli sauce, and mayonnaise there is 1 g carbohydrates per tablespoon. The fat burning quotient is about 5.0. If you reduce the amount of chilli sauce, the values improve.

Pesto

Mix in a food processor:

- 100–200 ml (3.5–7 fl oz) fresh basil compacted leaves (this will be a lot of basil!)
- A handful of nuts of your choice; cashew nuts or pinyon pine nuts are good
- A sprinkling of parmesan cheese
- A few garlic cloves
- Salt
- A dash of olive oil

Then I run the food processor while I add more olive oil. I like a more liquid pesto. I taste it, and I am usually satisfied. If not, I add whatever seems to be lacking.

You don't have to limit yourself to basil. There are many other delicious herbs. You can actually make pesto from water lily leaves or ruccola. The world of botany is open for exploration. I use pesto as flavouring. Then you can ignore the carbohydrates, because a tablespoon contains around ½ g carbohydrates.

Wonderful Italian sauces

Italians know how to make good food. Here are some classic Italian sauces. I like to cook and am always open to new impulses!

Primavera

Ingredients:
- 150 g (5.3 oz) fresh asparagus
- 30 g (1 oz) butter
- 25 ml cream
- 60 g (2.1 oz) grated parmesan

Cut the asparagus into pieces of equal size. Melt the butter in a frying pan and add the asparagus, cream, and parmesan. Simmer until the asparagus is bright green and barely cooked. Season to taste with salt and pepper.

Alfredo

Ingredients:
- 90 g (3 oz) butter
- 150 g (5.3 oz) grated parmesan
- 30 ml cream
- 3 tbs chopped parsley

Melt the butter in a pan on low heat. Add parmesan and cream and bring to a boil while stirring. Turn down the heat and let the sauce simmer. Continue to stir while the sauce thickens. Add parsley and season to taste with salt and pepper.

Carbonara

Ingredients:
- 1 pkg bacon (in cubes or strips)
- 4 eggs
- 50 g (1.75 oz) grated parmesan
- 30 ml cream

Start by frying the bacon. Mix together eggs, parmesan, and cream in a bowl. Add the bacon to this mixture. Pour mixture into a frying pan and simmer for 1 minute. Season to taste with pepper.

Boscaiola

Ingredients:
- 1 pkg bacon
- 200 g (7 oz) mushrooms
- 60 ml cream
- 2 green onions
- 1 tbs chopped parsley

Fry the bacon and the mushrooms. Add a little cream, preferably with a wooden spoon, and don't let the bacon stick to the bottom of the pan. Add the rest of the cream and bring to boil on high heat. Boil for 15 minutes. The sauce should be so thick that it sticks to the back of the wooden spoon. Add green onions and garnish with parsley.

Gorgonzola sauce

Ingredients:
- 200 g (7 oz) gorgonzola
- 20 g (¾ oz) butter

- 1 celery stalk, chopped
- 30 ml cream
- 250 g (8.75 oz) ricotta, stirred to even consistency

Cut the gorgonzola into small cubes. Melt the butter in a pan, add the celery, and sauté for 2 minutes. Add the cream, ricotta, and gorgonzola. Season to taste with pepper. Bring the sauce to a boil on low heat and let it simmer for a few minutes.

My favourite dressings

What is the real difference between a dressing and a cold sauce? There may be a scientific analysis of this somewhere, but for me the difference is consistency. Add liquid to one of my cold sauces and you have a dressing!

For the sake of simplicity I include the dressings I commonly use. This is to help you avoid shop-bought dressings. I use two dressings: a classic French dressing and a dressing based on mayonnaise.

Classic French dressing

This is how the French make a classic vinaigrette. This simple dressing suits almost all salads and is a necessary ingredient in many cold dishes.

According to the book you do the following:

1. Mix 1 tsp Dijon mustard in 10 ml vinegar.
2. Mix in 40 ml oil, a little at a time.
3. Add salt and pepper.

Or:

If I am pressed for time, I put all the ingredients in a jar and shake it well. This works. 2–3 tbs French dressing provides about 0.5 g carbohydrates, and the fat burning quotient is nearly 50! If you buy French dressing in the shop it can contain ten times more carbohydrates.

You should make everything you can from scratch. This is especially true for sauces and dressings. The only exception is shop-bought, low sugar mayonnaise.

Mayonnaise dressing

When I want a visible and "friendly" dressing, I use mayonnaise as a basis, preferably one that I have made myself. I often mix it with crème fraîche and spike it with some Dijon mustard, and I always add lemon juice or vinegar. The second seasoning is garlic. I generally use this kind of dressing on fish and seafood.

I use herbs according to need and desire. If I am making a fish salad, I often use tarragon; if it is a tomato salad, I will probably use basil. Salads that contain meat call for rosemary, oregano, or thyme, all according to what sounds good to me at the time. Sometimes I add a little water to get a thinner consistency.

Normally I avoid shop-bought sauces, but I do buy real mayonnaise on occasion. The 2 g carbohydrates per 100 g mayonnaise is acceptable. A dressing should contain something sour, and mayonnaise satisfies that requirement. If I can use less lemon, I save carbohydrates.

Crème fraîche goes very nicely with mayonnaise. Therefore I use it often, even though it adds some tenths of a gram of carbohydrates. If I need to cut down on carbohydrates I can find other solutions. Or just eat a smaller portion. Our ancestors didn't eat dressing!

A simple mayonnaise dressing

Take for example:
- 4 tbs mayonnaise (containing at most 2 g carbohydrates per 100 g)

- 2 tbs crème fraîche
- 1 tbs freshly squeezed lemon juice
- 1 tsp Dijon mustard
- 5 ml water
- Garlic, oregano, salad spices, Tabasco, or whatever you want

Put everything into a jar and shake well. The result is 200 ml of dressing containing a total of 3 g carbohydrates. That may sound like a lot, but you aren't going to eat 20 ml of dressing. If you limit your dressing to 4 tbs on a salad, it contains less than 1 g carbohydrates.

Mixed blue cheese dressing

Blue cheese is an excellent flavouring for a dressing. It is not free from carbohydrates, but the taste is concentrated and a small portion will suffice. Leif Mannerström is a top chef in Sweden. This is what he does:

- 100 g (3.5 oz) blue cheese
- 1 garlic clove
- 2 tsp white wine vinegar
- 150 ml sour cream
- Salt and pepper
- 1 tsp freshly squeezed lemon juice

Leif puts all the ingredients in a food processor and makes a creamy sauce with 200 kcal per portion, 2.6 g carbohydrates, and a fat burning quotient of 3.3.

I substitute the sour cream with crème fraîche and add a dash of water. Then I have less than 2 g carbohydrates and a fat burning quotient of 5.

Hamburger dressing

Hamburgers are a good food in the GI-Zero! program provided that you don't eat the bread! A quick dressing can be made with shop-bought mayonnaise and some rock salt or gherkins and onions. Colour and zing come with a little ground bell pepper and Tabasco. Some people like chilli sauce, but I don't. However, I never say no to the Indonesian chilli paste *sambal oelek*.

Herb butter

Butter tastes good with almost everything. I let it melt on food, I melt it for cheese soufflé, and I pour it over meat. In a crisis, I use a cheese knife to make slices of cold butter to put on meat, crush a garlic clove, and add some lemon pepper or herb salt.

Garlic butter, parsley butter, and other similar variations need no recipe. You slice the butter into a bowl, 100–200 g (3.5 – 7 oz), and let it soften. Then you mix in garlic, finely chopped parsley, tarragon, or whatever you want. A little salt and pepper is good. And I like lemon juice. Then I let the butter stiffen in the refrigerator.

Simple herb butter

Mix together butter, herbs, lemon juice, chopped parsley, and 1 tsp Worcestershire sauce (this is a classic ingredient in many herb butters).

All herb butters are best if they are made with melted butter, but that is seldom the case when I am doing the cooking. Don't be afraid to add too many herbs. Let the butter stiffen, rolled in some baking paper. Then you can cut nice slices to put on the dish.

Anchovy butter

I love anchovies. This spiced fish gives a wonderful flavour to many foods. Butter and cream sauces are just a few examples. When I make anchovy butter, I do it properly.

I brown the butter carefully to remove the water. Then I put it in the refrigerator to stiffen, and then mix it with anchovies, capers, and lemon juice. A good handful of chopped chives heightens the taste and appearance even more.

If you want an easier version, finely chop the anchovies, mix them with butter in a bowl, and season to taste. This works too.

The anchovy is a strong-tasting fish, so you should proceed carefully. First try 100–200 g (3.5 – 7 oz) butter, 3–4 anchovy fillets, some tbs capers, and a bunch of chives. The next time you can adjust the proportions until you have discovered your favourite butter.

Smoked herring butter

Substitute cleaned and crushed smoked herrings for the anchovies. A few drops of Worcestershire sauce are also good. This is excellent with grilled fish.

Horseradish butter

Add 1 tbs finely grated horseradish to 100 g (3.5 oz) butter and a dash of salt. Delicious on grilled fish.

Sandefjord butter

Reduce cream to half on low heat. Turn off the heat and add twice as much butter. Perhaps also some parsley and lemon juice. When the butter has melted, whisk until it is fluffy with a mild flavour. Suits white fish very well.

Simple béarnaise butter

Béarnaise sauce gets its flavour from tarragon, vinegar, and shallots. The same combination can be used in a herb butter.

Mix:
- 200 g (7 oz) butter
- 2 tsp finely chopped shallots
- 2 tsp dried tarragon
- 2 tbs chopped parsley

More advanced béarnaise butter

Ingredients:
- 2 finely chopped shallots
- 5 ml white wine vinegar
- 1 tbs dried tarragon
- 3 egg yolks
- 500 g (1 lb 2 oz) butter, room temperature
- 15 ml finely chopped parsley

Instructions:
1. Boil the shallots in the vinegar. Add tarragon.
2. Turn off the heat and beat in the egg yolks.
3. Blend mixture with butter and parsley in a blender.
4. Roll into greaseproof paper and refrigerate.

Roquefort butter

Mix butter with a good piece of Roquefort. About two parts butter and one part cheese works well. A dash of calvados provides a little zing. Season carefully; there is a lot of flavour in the cheese.

Chanterelle butter

Chanterelle butter is one of my favourites. It adds an excellent flavour to fried and grilled meat. The idea is simple. You steam the chanterelles, soak them in butter, add salt, and mix with more butter. A drop of lemon juice if you like. Parsley adds to the appearance.

It is important to steam as much water as possible out of the fresh mushrooms. If you don't do this, you will get a watery, boring butter. When you are finished steaming the mushrooms, let them simmer in butter for 20–30 minutes. I add salt carefully, let the mushrooms cool, and then I put everything in the blender with more butter. One to two litres of fresh chanterelles and a pound of butter works well. I taste, add more salt if necessary, and run the blender again.

Chanterelle butter can stay in the refrigerator for many weeks, or some months in the freezer. I am not sure, because it never lasts that long in my house!

Whiskey butter

I haven't tried this yet, so I would really like to hear what you think.

Mix 100 g (3.5 oz) butter with 30 ml whiskey, freshly chopped rosemary, salt and pepper. This butter should be delicious on grilled meat.

Normally I don't include recipes that I haven't tried, but the combination of whiskey and rosemary sounds very right.

Other good dressings

You don't necessarily need to use butter as a basis. Mayonnaise, whipped cream, crème fraîche, and sour cream can be combined and seasoned in a multitude of ways. Horseradish cream can be purchased as well.

Another horseradish cream

Combine two parts mayonnaise and one part crème fraîche. Mix in a good grated cheese and season to taste with horseradish. Great on roast beef and fish.

The simplest cheese dressing

Mix grated cheese with crème fraîche and season with cayenne pepper. Tastes good in all soups.

The simplest fish dressing

Crème fraîche with red caviar, onions, and lemon juice suits all kinds of fish. Substitute caviar from a tube for the red caviar, and you can eat it with chicken or entrecôte. At least according to a famous chef!

Some good appetisers

It is summer as I write this book. Summer is a time when it is natural to think of light, delicious appetisers to enjoy as hors d'œuvres or as a small meal when warm meals are somehow less appealing.

Summer salad

With shrimp, eggs, and mayonnaise you can always make a nutritious meal. Crème fraîche can be used to lighten the mayonnaise. Dijon mustard and lemon juice will add zest to the taste. Red caviar, whitefish caviar or capelin caviar are good accompaniments, but you can do without. Tinned asparagus is a vegetable that you can eat as much of as you like, and also suits this salad well.

Instructions:

1. Peel two pounds of shrimp. Set 100 g (3.5 oz) shrimp aside. Distribute the rest on a plate.
2. Place halved hardboiled eggs among the shrimp.
3. Prepare a mixture of mayonnaise, crème fraîche, and caviar. I use equal amounts of each. Season with 1–2 tsp Dijon mustard, some minced onion, and lemon juice. Salt and coarsely ground pepper are also great. Put the dressing between the eggs or on top, as you prefer.
4. Sprinkle the remaining shrimp over the salad and garnish

with fresh dill. A few lemon wedges here and there look good.

Let us suppose that you eat 200 g (7 oz) shrimp, 1 egg, and a tablespoon each of mayonnaise, crème fraîche, and caviar. This equals about 400 kcal and 3.5 g carbohydrates. If you don't add onion, you save half a gram carbohydrate. Fat burning quotient: 1.0.

Pesto-marinated mozzarella

For the pesto you need:

- 50 g (1.75 oz) fresh basil leaves
- 3 tbs nuts (walnuts, almonds, etc.)
- 3 tbs grated parmesan
- 2 garlic cloves
- Olive oil
- Salt

Combine the dry ingredients in a food processor until you have a fine-grained mixture. Add olive oil to taste and desired consistency. Put the pesto in a bowl and add 300 g (10.5 oz) mozzarella in cubes. Mix carefully, cover with clingfilm and put in the refrigerator for about 2 hours.

If you use 100 ml (3.5 fl oz) olive oil in the pesto and divide the amount into 4 portions, you have 500 kcal and barely 4 g carbohydrates per portion. Fat burning quotient: 2.0.

Anchovy paste

Traditional Swedish *smörgås* or open-faced sandwiches often consist of anchovies or smoked herring. Anchovies contain as much sugar as herring, but you eat fewer of them. Therefore I often use anchovies. Warm-smoked herring contains no carbohydrates and you can eat as many of them as you like. Brined herring must be avoided until we have achieved our weight loss because they are sugar bombs.

Finely chop:
- 10 anchovy fillets
- 1 hardboiled egg
- 1 onion

Mix ingredients in a little bowl or a teacup. Pour a little anchovy brine in and mix well. Turn upside down on a plate and garnish with parsley.

This paste is a delectable salty teaser in the heat of summer. You can eat it in group 4+ and 2+. Divide it into 4 portions, and you get 4 g carbohydrates. Fat burning quotient: 0.5. Continue the meal with barbecued steak and anchovy butter, keeping you under 6 g.

Smoked herring in mayonnaise

Warm-smoked herring is carbohydrate-free. Mayonnaise is almost carbohydrate-free, even if you buy it in the grocery shop. Eggs contain very few carbohydrates. Here you have the ingredients for a dish with an excellent fat burning quotient.

Suggested *ingredients:*
- 10 tbs mayonnaise
- 2 tbs cream
- 3 cleaned herrings
- 2 hardboiled eggs
- Lots of dill

1. Mix the mayonnaise and the cream.
2. Mix the herring, mayonnaise mixture, and sliced egg in a bowl. Add mayonnaise.
3. Garnish with dill and refrigerate. Serve chilled.

If you divide the recipe into four portions, each portion will be 500 kcal and less than 1 g carbohydrates. Fat burning quotient: 5.3! This little summer dish can be eaten in all of the groups.

Smoked herring is also good in scrambled eggs. Two smoked herrings and a small portion of scrambled eggs provides 440 kcal and 1.8 g carbohydrates. Fat burning quotient: 1.3.

Salmon is an approved food

Salmon is a good food for the GI-Zero! program. It is a fatty and healthy fish that works well with low carbohydrate creamed spinach or a portion of coleslaw.

100 g (3.5 oz) salmon contains about 200 calories, no matter how it is prepared. Fat burning quotient: 0.6. The high protein level reduces the quotient. Carbohydrates aren't present.

100 g (3.5 oz) parboiled salmon with Mervis' spinach scramble provides 350 kcal and 1.8 g carbohydrates. Fat burning quotient: 0.9. Substitute 100 g (3.5 oz) coleslaw for the spinach and you have 380 kcal, 3.8 g carbohydrates, and a fat burning quotient of 1.0.

Spinach pannacotta with smoked salmon

Ingredients:
- About 100 g (3.5 oz) smoked salmon, sliced
- 1.5 sheets of gelatine
- 150 ml cream
- 150 g (5.25 oz) frozen chopped spinach
- 100 ml Turkish yoghurt
- Lemon zest
- 1 tbs freshly squeezed lemon juice

Instructions:
1. Soften gelatine in cold water, for about 5 minutes.
2. Bring cream and spinach to a boil.
3. Squeeze the gelatine and melt it in the warm cream mixture.
4. Add yoghurt, lemon zest, and lemon juice.
5. Shred salmon and stir into cream mixture.
6. Divide into four bowls and let stiffen in refrigerator. Garnish with a little smoked salmon, dill, and lemon wedges.

If we count this as four portions, each portion contains 250 calories and 3 g carbohydrates. Fat burning quotient: 1.7. This dish contains many good vitamins and minerals as well.

My mayonnaise eggs

Mayonnaise eggs are a French classic. This dish can be eaten with your homemade mayonnaise (see the recipe on page 43). Use warm, recently hardboiled eggs. They should not be at refrigerator temperature, and the yolk should be a little soft. Mix with your own mayonnaise and a dash of Dijon mustard.

I usually crush a few green olives in a garlic press. I discovered this when I read about an olive mayonnaise somewhere. I had no recipe, but the garlic press works just fine. You can follow up by crushing a garlic clove!

With an egg and a dollop of mayonnaise, this is a great appetiser. Some bitter, green leaves of lettuce help the appearance. I often eat two eggs and have some more mayonnaise. And maybe a glass of muscatel wine. Then I really feel like it is summer.

With two eggs, a good amount of mayonnaise, and some endive you have 500 calories and 1.5 g carbohydrates. Fat burning quotient: 3.

Soused herring fillets stuffed with dill or parsley

A Swede can't imagine a more summery food than bread-crumbed Baltic herring fillets stuffed with dill or parsley and soused in an old-fashioned vinegar. Breadcrumbed fish sounds like a catastrophe, but there is less bread involved than you might think. Normal breadcrumbed herring fillets contain about 4 g carbohydrates per 100 g (3.5 oz) portion. This is perfectly acceptable in groups 4+ and 2+. If you breadcrumb them in crushed deep-fried bacon rinds you can actually make an extremely carbohydrate-poor dish that works even in the 8+ group.

But here we are going to eat 100 g (3.5 oz) regular stuffed herring fillets and add a good dollop of mayonnaise mixed with crème fraîche and Dijon mustard. Or some other good dressing. We have to watch out for the vinegar and onions, for that is where the carbohydrates are. A standard portion of 100 g (3.5 oz) regular stuffed herring fillets contains about 450 kcal and less than 3 g carbohydrates. Fat burning quotient: 2.0.

What about brined herring and potatoes?

Unfortunately the answer is no. I have done the calculations on this classic dish over and over again, but there is no good solution. Of course you can eat this pleasant dish and drown your bad conscience in liquor. But don't expect to feel great the following day!

The problem is that the herring is in sugar brine. Calculate 20 % sugar in normal brined herring. If you read the numbers on the tin or jar, you will find even higher values, but these numbers include the brine.

Brined herring is a little better, but not good enough. Fifty grams brined herring (1 fillet) with sour cream and chives contains 7 g carbohydrates. And that doesn't include the potatoes. Eat even a little spring potato and you push the limit of 9 g!

Put a knob of butter on that little potato, and you have a dish that tastes like summer. It contains less than 300 kcal and 9 g carbohydrates. Fat burning quotient: 1.3.

Which vegetables are best?

The answer is simple. The best vegetables are those that grow above ground. They contain less starch and therefore the weakest fat storage signals. We must avoid starch. Starch is composed of large, complex glucose molecules. As soon as these molecules come into contact with saliva, they break down and send signals about fat storage. Starch is a carbohydrate, and carbohydrates turn fat metabolism off!

The list below is for the 4+ group. It shows how many vegetables lie within the limit of 6 g carbohydrates. In other words, group 4+ members can eat these vegetables as side dishes to meats. Those in group 2+ can eat even more.

Group 8+ are my fakirs. They should eat as strictly as possible and put all their efforts into losing 4 stone (25 kg). Once they have lost that much, they can eat more flexibly. Decorative leaves are permitted, perhaps also a creamed spinach, a Florida salad (see page 126) or a frittata (see page 74) with coffee.

The only root vegetables that I can recommend are winter radishes and common radishes. If you think that they are good, you are in luck.

You can save some carbohydrates if you want, but you shouldn't eat all your carbohydrates in one meal. That can be enough to wake cravings in someone who is very sensitive to carbohydrates.

The table indicates that 63 g (2.2 oz) cooked carrots contains 6 g carbohydrates. Sixty-three grams (2.2 oz) is not very much at all. However, you can eat ten times that amount of cooked spinach. Use the list wisely and it will be easier to eat food that people around you accept. They really want to see green leaves on your plate!

Six grams carbohydrates equals the following amounts of vegetables:

- 60 g (2.1 oz) parsnips
- 63 g (2.2 oz) cooked carrots
- 65 g (2.2 oz) cooked beets
- 93 g (3.3 oz) cooked swede
- 100 g (3.5 oz) yellow onion
- 100 g (3.5 oz) sugar peas
- 120 g (4.2 oz) cooked leek
- 125 g (4.4 oz) red bell pepper
- 134 g (4.7 oz) aubergine
- 150 g (5.3 oz) avocado (about 2 halves)
- 155 g (5.5 oz) tomatoes
- 160 g (5.6 oz) cooked cabbage
- 175 g (6.2 oz) cooked cauliflower
- 195 g (6.9 oz) mangelwurzel (mangold)
- 195 g (6.9 oz) green pepper
- 200 g (7 oz) cooked broccoli
- 200 g (7 oz) French beans
- 240 g (8.5 oz) sauerkraut
- 240 g (8.5 oz) winter radishes
- 260 g (9.2 oz) cooked asparagus
- 270 g (9.5 oz) iceberg lettuce
- 285 g (10 oz) courgette
- 300 g (10.6 oz) gherkins

- 300 g (10.6 oz) radishes (75 radishes!)
- 375 g (13.2 oz) fresh spinach
- 600 g (1 lb 5 oz) tinned asparagus
- 675 g (1 lb 8 oz) cooked spinach (The amount of spinach is amazing, but my nutritional program confirms it. I guess I have to start eating more spinach!)

Study the list carefully. Choose a vegetable on the list that you like, and learn to prepare it in different ways. Then the journey towards your goal will be easier.

Bread and foods similar to bread

My general attitude towards bread is that we should avoid it as much as possible. For those who are overweight, there is a simple rule: bread turns our fat metabolism off! If we maintain the habit of eating bread, we will always run the risk of eating the wrong kind of bread when nothing else is available.

There are types of bread that are better than others. The previously mentioned sourdough rye bread is an example. However, there really are no healthy breads available in grocery stores. If you are going to eat a sandwich, the sliced meats and cheeses should be on something that you have baked yourself. Here are some recipes:

Cheese bread that tastes good with everything
This is a classic recipe that originally comes from the Polish physician and author Jan Kwasniewski. Cheese bread can accompany everything.

You can make sandwiches with it, a remarkably good pizza, or the Swedish specialty *smörgåstorta* (a kind of salty cake-like sandwich). You can bake cheese bread in a long pan and roll it. With mozzarella it tastes like a pancake, and with a matured cheese it has a bite. The breads are great for picnics and perfect for tacos. Your imagination is the limit.

And best of all: there are fewer than 1 g carbohydrates per piece!

For a large batch, 35–50 pieces, you use:
- 2 containers of cottage cheese (600 g, 1 lb 5 oz). Let the cottage cheese drain in a sieve, or press out the liquid.
- About 900 g (2 lb) of grated cheese. Select a fat-rich cheese.
- 15 eggs, separated into yolks and whites
- Seasoning dependent on the type of cheese. I like basil or oregano.

For a smaller batch, 9–10 pieces (takes up one baking sheet):
- ½ container cottage cheese (150 g, 5.3 oz)
- 200 g (7 oz) grated cheese
- 4 eggs
- Seasoning

Instructions:

Beat the egg whites until stiff – add a dash of salt to make them really stiff. If the egg whites aren't really stiff, the bread will look like an omelette.

Mash the cottage cheese and the egg yolks with a hand-held immersion blender or a spoon. Mix in the grated cheese with a spatula. Season with salt, white pepper, and fresh herbs, according to your taste. Even pizza seasoning will work. Fold the beaten whites into the mixture.

The bread batter is ready. If you intend to make something really satisfying, you can mix in finely chopped ham or fried bacon in the batter. But that usually is part of an advanced course. The first time around you should just make normal cheese bread.

Cover the baking sheet with baking paper. Portion out the batter with a spoon. There will be 9–10 portions with the small batch, and four or five cooking sheets full with the large batch. Remember that the breads expand during baking. Bake at 175 °C for about 20 minutes until they are golden brown.

The bread can be eaten on its own, or with salami, cheese, ham, or mayonnaise. They are also perfect bases for mini-pizzas. Try to keep a supply in the freezer, separated by baking paper. Grab one or two, add some sliced meat or pizza sauce, grate some cheese over it, and put them into the oven briefly.

One cheese bread alone provides about 100 kcal, with 8 g protein and 7 g fat. Less than 1 g carbohydrate per piece! The fat burning quotient is 0.76, but will increase to about 1.0 if you add sliced meat or cheese. Add a teaspoon of mayonnaise and you have a fat burning quotient of 1.3. A satisfying open-faced sandwich with 20 g cheese, three slices of salami, and a few tomato slices provides 250 kcal, with 17 g protein, 20 g fat, and 2.5 g carbohydrates. 20 g fat divided by 19.5 g of protein and carbohydrates yields a fat burning quotient of 1.

Less than 1 g carbohydrate per bread!

Delicious cheese and spinach frittata

You will find different versions of this recipe on the internet – it is delicious. Frittatas can accompany many different main dishes, or be eaten as snacks or a substitute for cake with your coffee. You can use nettles or mushrooms instead of spinach if you like, or make the frittata as a cheese muffin. Exact measurements aren't critical, I just follow my gut feeling.

I use a muffin tin. Just be sure to grease the tin thoroughly – the cheese can make a sticky mess!

Beat together:
- 6 eggs
- Chopped parsley, at least 50 g (1.75 oz)

- 1 tsp herbs, such as basil or oregano
- A few drops of Tabasco

Add cheese and green leaves, for example:
- 1 pkg (300 g, 10.5 oz) chopped spinach
- 60 g (2 oz) grated parmesan
- 100 g (3.5 oz) grated cheese (NB! Grate the cheese yourself. Many of the packaged grated cheeses aren't really cheese. Quite a few are a mixture of oil and skimmed milk, and are marketed as heart-friendly!)
- A container of cottage cheese (300 g, 10.5 oz)

Bake about 20 minutes at 200 °C. Eat warm or cold. Keeps well in the refrigerator. A frittata contains 130 kcal. and 1.2 g carbohydrate. Fat burning quotient: 0.64.

Gojkan's versatile bread

This bread works instead of crips, crisp bread, or as the base for a *smörgåstorta*. Can also be used as a pizza base!

Gojkan calls it "a wonderfully easy bread that my husband loves!"

Ingredients:
- 3 eggs
- 300 g (10.5 oz) ground deep-fried bacon rinds
- 300 g (10.5 oz) tasty, fat-rich cheese, preferably grated
- Salt or season to taste (I prefer garlic)

Instructions:
Mix ingredients and portion the batter out onto baking paper. Press each piece of bread flat. These will not expand during baking.

Bake at 275 °C, a few minutes on each side, until golden brown.

Leave to cool. To keep crispy, don't store in a closed container. If you are going to use them in a *smörgåstårta,* wrap them in clingfilm.

The entire recipe provides 3–4 g carbohydrates. That is not a lot per slice of bread. Fat burning quotient: 1.

Another bread by the same baker

Ingredients:
- ½ pkg dry yeast
- 3 eggs
- 100 ml (3.5 fl oz) Greek or Turkish yoghurt (with 10% fat)
- 200 ml (7 fl oz) water or cream
- 200–300 g (7–10.5 oz) ground deep-fried bacon rinds
- 100 g (3.5 oz) grated fat-rich cheese
- ½ tsp salt
- 2 grated garlic cloves

Instructions:
1. Mix ingredients and turn into a well-greased bread pan. Leave to rise for 15 minutes.
2. Bake at 225 °C for about 35 minutes. Turn out of pan and cool on rack.

My comments:

I haven't tried this bread because I don't want to re-awaken my cravings for bread. Bread made me fat. However, the contents of this bread are good. Baked with cream there will be about 1 g carbohydrate per slice and a fat burning quotient of 1.7. If you use water there will be 0.7 g carbohydrate and a fat burning quotient of 0.8.

Cheese in the oven

You can bake grated cheese as it is. Crispy, crunchy and good for you. You can mix eggs and cheese in all combinations to eat with soup. You can add 1 tbs cream per egg and bake the mixture in muffin tins. Your imagination is the only limiting factor.

Tilda's chicken crisps

Normal snacks are not good for you, but Tilda's chicken crisps are okay. Zero carbohydrates!

Instructions:
1. Fry up some chicken fillets. Season carefully.
2. Cool, and cut into very thin slices.
3. Put in an oven pan under low temperature in the oven. Dry until crispy. Perfect as healthy crisps when everyone else is eating snacks.

Coconut pancakes – mostly for coconut lovers!

I found this recipe on a Norwegian low-carb website. The pancakes are a good solution to a surplus of spare egg whites. For a proper pancake that will serve two people:
– 5 egg whites
– 100 g (3.5 oz) coconut flakes
– Butter

1. Beat the eggs until stiff. A dash of salt makes this easier.
2. Add coconut.
3. Fry on both sides in melted butter. I make one big thick pancake in a large frying pan. You can make two small ones if you prefer. Fry until golden brown. Don't burn the pancake; it does not behave like an ordinary pancake.

Some people like this pancake, some think it is awful. I haven't quite made up my mind. I like coconut, but I haven't found a good way to use this pancake. I wonder if it would taste good with red caviar, onions, and sour cream? Try it and send me a report!

Half a pancake contains about 500 kcal and 2.6 g carbohydrates. The fat burning quotient runs to about 3–4 depending on the amount of butter. No matter the taste, we can eat this pancake and feel like we are taking a step on the road to good health.

Pirjo's cheese meringues

An alternative use for your surplus egg whites are Pirjo's cheese meringues.

1. Beat egg whites until stiff.
2. Add a few tablespoons grated cheese per egg white.
3. Distribute batter on baking paper. Bake at 100 °C until dry. This usually takes 30 minutes.

Three meringues contain about 1 g carbohydrates. Fat burning quotient: 0.5.

Some small, medium and large sins!

Those of us who follow THE SCANDINAVIAN DIET usually avoid fruit, sweets and desserts. Such temptations make losing weight more difficult and maintain our sugar cravings. However, if we decide to sin now and then, we should select less damaging alternatives.

Sins do the least harm when they are isolated from other foods. The best time is late in the evening. If you feel the need for fruit, you should eat it early in the morning. But then you should avoid eating for a few hours. Fruit releases fat storage signals!

Cheater's ice chocolate

Melt equal parts coconut oil and dark chocolate in a thick-bottomed pan. Add chopped nuts if you like. Pour into small paper cases and leave to cool. Or fill an ice cube tray; that works much more quickly.

Organic, cold-pressed coconut oil is best.

A 20 g piece contains 150 kcal and 4 g carbohydrates. The fat burning quotient is 3. I don't think that we should eat sweets but this sin is less serious because the fat is so healthy. Decide how big the sin is yourself.

Quick chocolate mousse

It is not possible to combine chocolate mousse, brownies, and ice cream substitutes with natural foods. We are not designed to eat such things. However, sometimes we have guests and we may want to eat the same thing we are serving them. This creamed chocolate mousse for ourselves but a mousse that really tastes like chocolate for our guests.

Mix a little melted chocolate in stiffly whipped cream. I use a lot of cream and only a little chocolate. Add grated orange peel to taste and refrigerate. That is your mousse! Maria Tauson, a well-known internet chef, whips an egg into the warm chocolate. That is probably good, but it doesn't work as well when you only melt a single square of chocolate.

Chocolate mousse and similar delights are minefields! Suppose you use 10 g chocolate (90 % cocoa) to 100 ml (3.5 fl oz) cream and 1 tsp grated orange peel. That is just a hint of chocolate, but even so the portion contains 7.4 g carbohydrates, over half of which come from that little bit of chocolate!

If you use the normal amount, or 50 g (2 oz) chocolate to 100 ml (3.5 fl oz) cream, you have 700 kcal and 22 g carbohydrates. The fat burning quotient is 2.2, but that doesn't help when there are so many carbohydrates. The fat burning quotient depends on a low intake of carbohydrates.

The GI con artists say that you can eat some pieces of dark chocolate every night. Maybe you're beginning to understand that this can't be true. With THE SCANDINAVIAN DIET we normalise our body weight. When we have accomplished this, we can find out how many sweets we can tolerate.

Pannacotta with sugar

My friend, physician Bjørn H, sent me this recipe for pannacotta, a little dessert that serves 6 people.

Bring 600 ml (just over 1 pint) cream and 1 tbs sugar barely to a boil and set the mixture to cool. Add 1–2 sheets of gelatine to the cream, mix well, and pour into a tray. Refrigerate for at least 3 hours. Before serving, garnish with raspberries, fresh or frozen. Enjoy!

If you use the raspberries as a garnish, you can get away with 5–6 g carbohydrates per portion. Each portion contains 40 g fat, and that provides a fat burning quotient of 4.

Pannacotta with stevia

If you have decided to avoid sugar, stevia can be an alternative.

Instructions:

Bring 250 ml (9 fl oz) cream barely to a boil. Scrape in ½ vanilla pod (optional). Melt 1.5 sheets of gelatine. Put a few raspberries in a dish, pour the mixture over, and keep refrigerated. Top with raspberries before serving.

If we call this two portions, you can use about 50 g (2 oz) raspberries per portion to hold the carbohydrate total under 6 g.

Super simple pannacotta

1. Soften two sheets of gelatine
2. Bring 300 ml (11 fl oz) cream to a boil.
3. Remove from heat.
4. Mix in gelatine.
5. Pour into three small glasses and refrigerate.
6. Top with some raspberries before serving.

What you should always have in the house

One excuse that I find worse than all the others, is when a student says that they didn't have anything else to eat. This is supposed to explain why they ate a bag of crisps or a chocolate cake. Anyone who wants healthy food but doesn't have any in their kitchen, has decided to stay fat.

To avoid this terrible fate, you must remove all the rubbish food from your cupboards and fill them with healthy foods. If you have family members who want to eat rubbish food, make them keep it somewhere else and eat it in secret. It doesn't belong in your cupboard!

In the freezer:
- Ready-to-eat meals based on GI-Zero! recipes. Start from the bottom and build up a bank of healthy food by always making several more portions than you need. Usually I have enough food to last a month, long siege.
- Meat, fish, and poultry, also heart, liver, and kidneys. Avoid fast foods and commercially produced foods. They are full of sugar, starch, and chemicals.

In the refrigerator and the cupboard:

- Eggs! Pay more for good eggs. You can never eat too many eggs.
- Cheese of all kinds. The higher the fat content, the better.
- Bacon or salt pork
- Butter, coconut oil, olive oil
- Cream and crème fraîche
- Dijon mustard
- Sugar-free mayonnaise
- Mackerel in tomato sauce, tuna fish in oil
- Olives, all kinds
- Garlic and onions
- Some vegetables that grow above ground
- Lots of seasonings

Good to have on hand:

- Sour cream and cream cheese (like Philadelphia)
- Anchovies, sardines
- Chillies if you like
- Tabasco
- Worcestershire sauce

Not necessary:

- Sugar, flour, potatoes, bread, crisps, soda pop, and concentrated juice …

Some practical tips

Deep-fried bacon rinds can be used in many dishes. You can eat them like crisps, or you can grind them and use them in bread baking or as breadcrumbing.

Breadcrumbing with ground deep-fried bacon rinds

Do you want to eat breadcrumbed fish, without flour or ground bread? Then ground deep-fried bacon rinds are a good solution. And no, it won't make the fish taste like bacon. On a veal schnitzel this breadcrumbing is perfect!

Eat liver as medicine!

We should eat liver, heart, or kidney once a week. These are some of the healthiest foods around. A portion of beef liver (100 g, 3.5 oz) contains as many important nutrients as a bucket of organic vegetables. Unfortunately, liver is high in carbohydrates. Chicken liver is the exception. A simple solution is to eat liver in small doses like medicine.

Ten grams fried beef liver provides two recommended daily doses of vitamin A and six recommended daily doses of vitamin B_{12}. Vitamin B_{12} is a critical vitamin that is not present in the plant world. Every day I consume at least ten times the recommended daily dose.

Next time you prepare liver I suggest that you freeze some portions. Take them out of the freezer now and then and eat a piece. When you do this, you can stop taking your other vitamin pills.

A medical dose of liver (10 g) contains 0.5 g carbohydrates. If you don't have room for that, use chicken liver as medicine. It only contains 0.15 g carbohydrates.

Hearts!

Boil up some hearts (any kind) in a lot of water. Add salt and onions, bay leaf, and other seasonings to taste. Large hearts from cows and pigs – and even game if you can find them! – should simmer for about two hours. Allow to cool in the stock.

Cut the hearts in slices and eat them with Dijon mustard or horseradish cream made with cream or mayonnaise. Whatever you don't eat can be stored in the stock in the refrigerator.

Hearts from large animals contain no carbohydrates. Chicken hearts contain 0.8 g carbohydrates per 100 g. The fat burning quotient is low, 0.3–0.5. But hearts are excellent food. They don't contain vitamin A, but they provide good amounts of vitamin B, iron, phosphorus, and zinc. Hunters have known this since time immemorial. And they probably have other positive effects that we don't even know about.

If you like kidneys, they are good for you too. You have to eat more than 200 g (7 oz) to top 1 g carbohydrate. The nutritional benefit lies somewhere between livers and hearts.

Soaking salt bacon

When you have eaten according to THE SCANDINAVIAN DIET for a while, you will notice how your taste changes. Sweet foods taste sweeter, and salty foods taste saltier. The truth is that your natural sense of taste returns. This becomes a problem if you like bacon, because a lot of bacon is over-salted.

There are two solutions. You can switch to salt pork. Salt pork has more fat and less chemicals. Or you can soak bacon in water overnight. In the morning, you will see the chemicals in the water!

Press the water out of the bacon under running water and fry up as usual. It will be nearly free from salt.

Don't throw away any cheese!

Many people who eat according to THE SCANDINAVIAN DIET have a lot of cheese in their refrigerator. I belong to this group. When pieces of parmesan get too hard, I go through the refrigerator and gather up all the old pieces of different cheeses and run them through a food processor. If there isn't enough, I toss in some more. Then I run two parts cheese and one part butter in the processor. Cumin is a classic seasoning for this mixture.

The result is pot cheese. I eat it like a sweet. It can be stored in a stoneware crock.

A summary
of the 8+ program

The plate model for the 8+ group:

Three parts meat and one part fat. Green leaves as garnish.

Carbohydrate limit: 3 g carbohydrates per meal. 12 g carbohydrates per day.

This is the strict GI-Zero! program for those of you who weigh more than 8 stone (50 kg) too much, or those who have tried all other programs without sustainable results. GI-Zero! works for all seriously overweight people, provided they follow the program. If you hesitate to dedicate three months of your life to this program, choose another. Your results will not be as good, but perhaps you can lead a more normal life.

Pure GI-Zero! is no game, not something that you try for a week or two, but an active program for those of you who really want to change your life. You do the first evaluation after 3 months, and in the course of those 3 months you must not deviate from the program.

If all goes well, you continue the program until you have lost at least half of the weight you want to lose. If you have trouble following the program, it is better to choose the 4+ program. Then you can eat a moderate amount of salad now and then, and that alone makes life easier for many.

How do you know if you need pure GI-Zero?

8+ is a plan for people who are highly sensitive to carbo-hydrates; people who gain weight if they so much as look at a slice of whole wheat bread! I belong to this group, so I know they exist. Everyone in this group is insulin resistant. That means that their bodies release large amounts of insulin every time their blood sugar levels rise. At the same time as their insulin rises, their metabolism of fat turns off. They gain weight no matter what they eat. This is the reason why so many seriously overweight people fail to lose weight even on starvation diets. Yes, I know you don't have any sweets hiding in your desk drawer! Those of us who are hyper-sensitive to carbohydrates, don't have to.

If you belong to the 8+ group, you need to avoid un-necessary increases in your blood sugar levels. That is why your recommended food consists of meat and fat. Three parts meat and one part fat is ideal. Measured in terms of energy content, this means that you eat 15–20 percent pro-tein, 70–80 percent fat, and a maximum of 5 percent car-bohydrates. The high proportion of fat leads to high metab-olism of fat.

How I eat today

I have practiced the 8+ program throughout most of my weight loss process, but I am often asked how I eat today. The answer is that I eat approximately like I did before, but I add some vegetables every day. However, I only eat small portions of greens, and only vegetables that grow above ground. If I ate starch, for example carrots or potatoes, I would quickly gain weight again. Such is life for the carbo-hydrate sensitive. Hopefully you have more flexibility.

I don't have any special menus, and you can combine recipes in this group exactly as you please. In the beginning, you will probably be eating something different in the morning. Many do, but that habit has a tendency to disappear. After a few years on this diet most people eat the same kind of food no matter what time of the day it is.

But let's take a look at what one day could look like. I once sent this menu to someone who asked for advice. It is intended for men, but the principles are the same for women.

Breakfast:

Fried salt pork the way you like it. When the pork is almost ready, add:
- 1 egg
- 2–3 egg yolks
- A dash of cream

Mix with a spatula to make a fluffy omelette.

This breakfast provides 700 kcal and 2 g carbohydrates. Fat burning quotient: 1.7.

Lunch
(when you are hungry, not because it is noon):

- Lamb chops, as many as you want.
- Herb butter and broccoli cooked in butter (you can mix broccoli and cauliflower with cream and butter if you would like a mash).

This lunch provides 700 kcal and 2.5 g carbohydrates. Fat burning quotient: 1.1.

Dinner:

- A large, fat-rich piece of meat (meat or fish!) with herb butter and ratatouille. (Should this not be enough, the piece of meat is too small. Increase the meat portion.)

This dinner provides about 700 kcal and 7.5–15 g carbohydrates. Fat burning quotient: 0.9.

Total for the day:

About 2100 kcal, 12–20 g carbohydrates. Fat burning quotient: 1.2. Notice that I eat about the same amount every meal. After a large dinner I am seldom hungry in the morning. Then I skip breakfast, because you should only eat when you are hungry. I never eat between meals.

Comments:

The nutritional calculations I did just now was for the purposes of this book. I only calculate for the benefit of others, not for myself. I eat until I am satisfied and let my body take care of the rest. I have maintained my new reduced weight by eating this way. When I weighed 22 stone 12 (145 kg), I ate less than today, but I ate food that continually sent out fat storage signals.

Today I probably eat like the 4+ group even though I eat more carbohydrates in the evening. On the other hand, I eat fewer carbohydrates over the course of the day. I have no need to eat like the 2+ group. I could eat like this group, but my body doesn't demand that kind of food. It is highly likely that I will continue to eat this way for the rest of my life. I am 65, so I have about 30 years left. You can get old and healthy on a natural diet!

If I want to lose weight, I drop the vegetables. Then I have a daily intake of a few carbohydrates. If I want to gain weight, I eat fruit. Last spring I tried to eat 3–4 sharon fruits every day. This fruit represents 60–70 g carbohydrates. Otherwise I continued to eat as usual, but I gained up to 4.5 lb per week for several weeks. Fruit sends out fat storage signals!

Recipes for 8+

Minced meat can be served in a multitude of variations. We can add eggs, cream, crème fraîche, or mayonnaise. We can add stock or water. We can season with pepper sauce or Dijon mustard. We can stuff the minced meat with different cheeses. We can pack it in bacon and fry it in a pan or bake it in the oven. The only thing that we can't do is to add things to the minced meat like breadcrumbs, rice, potatoes, oatmeal, or anything else that comes into conflict with our weight losing process.

Let's look at some diet meat patties of a more appetising character.

Fakir steak à la Wallenberg

Wallenberg is a classic Swedish luxury dish made of minced veal, cream, and egg yolks. Perfect food with a fat burning quotient of 2. If you use pork mince, it is considerably less expensive and has an even better fat burning quotient.

I usually make a large portion, but you must do as you please. The original recipe calls for one egg yolk and 100 ml (3.5 fl oz) cream per 100 g (3.5 oz) minced meat. I think this is too sticky, so instead I use one egg yolk and 50 ml cream per 100 g minced meat.

Ingredients:
- 1 kg (2.2 lb) pork mince
- 50 ml (2 fl oz) cream
- 10 egg yolks
- Salt and pepper to taste

Instructions:
Mix the cream into the pork mince with a large spoon. Add cream gradually. Add egg yolks gradually. Season. Test fry a piece to see if you have achieved the mild, creamy taste.

This is a large portion that will make at least 10 large patties (I usually make 20). Deglaze the pan with stock or wine, mix in a little cream. This will reduce to a good sauce.

One large patty contains 500 kcal and 1.5 g carbohydrates. Fat burning quotient is a whopping 2.2!

Meat patties with feta cheese

This is a simple recipe that we often make in our home. It is always tasty, and it is easy to make an incredible sauce from the pan drippings.

Instructions:
- Mix minced beef with egg, some chopped olives, and feta cheese. Add a few tablespoons of cream. Season as you like. Pepper is necessary, but the feta and olives contain salt.
- Test fry a thin piece to check the seasoning.
- Shape into large, flat patties and fry in butter and a little oil.
- Deglaze the pan with a little stock, add cream, and reduce to a cream sauce. A few drops of soy sauce will add colour.

150 g (5 oz) of minced beef without sauce provides 350 kcal and almost 1 g carbohydrates. The fat burning quotient is

1.1. A few tablespoons of sauce increase the carbohydrates to 2 g and the fat burning quotient to over 1.5.

You have room for a few green leaves.

Bacon meatloaf!

I make my meatloaf without a recipe, but the ingredients for a normal meatloaf are as follows:

- 1 kg (2.2 lb) mixed minced meat
- 1 pkg fried bacon, crumbled
- 1 chopped onion
- 2 garlic cloves
- 2 eggs
- 200 ml (7 fl oz) cream
- 1 tbs Dijon mustard
- Butter
- Salt, pepper, and other seasonings

Instructions:

1. If this is going to be a meatloaf, I crumble the fried bacon into a bowl. I mix the mustard into the cream, and add this to the rest of the ingredients in the bowl. I grease the pan and then press the meat mixture into it. Bake at 175°C for about an hour. You can push sticks of cheese into the meat or put olives and feta cheese in the minced meat. Use your imagination!
2. Instead of crumbling up the bacon, you can wrap strips of bacon around the minced meat, as a kind of a protective layer. This will make a moist, juicy meatloaf, and it will be easy to see when the meatloaf is done.

Cut the meatloaf into 10 slices. Each slice will provide 300 kcal and 1.3 carbohydrates. In the 8+ group you can have 2 slices and some pan drippings without surpassing 3 carbohydrates. Fat burning quotient: 1.1.

If you are in the 4+ group, you can add a cream sauce and some cooked broccoli.

Salisbury steak with onion flavour

One normal portion of fried onions (10 g) contains about 3 g carbohydrates. If you don't eat all the onions, you can eat this delicious dish even if you are in the 8+ group. The onion flavour is still there!

Salisbury steak should really be made from pure minced beef, but I use minced beef mixed with some cream to increase the fat burning quotient. Pure minced pork also works well, but the dish takes on a different character.

Instructions:
1. Slice onion and brown in butter and oil on medium heat.
2. When the onion is translucent, season the meat with salt and pepper and shape flat patties in the size you like.
3. Remove the onions, turn up the heat and fry the patties on both sides. Minced beef will be done before minced pork.
4. Put warm patties on a warm plate.
5. Deglaze the pan with stock or water. Stir. Add onions and reduce.
6. Pour onion sauce over patties.

All the carbohydrates are in the onions. Without onions you are down to zero carbohydrates. With a few onions on each patty you are close to your critical limit of 3 g carbohydrates. The fat burning quotient depends on the type of mince you use. Normal minced beef has a fat burning quotient of about 1, pork mince has 1.5.

Cheese-stuffed minced meat patties

As you will see in these different recipes, I like combinations of cheese and minced beef. Here is yet another variation, cheese-stuffed minced meat patties.

Ingredients:
- Mixed ground meat, beef and pork
- Eggs
- Cream
- Cheese, preferably blue cheese
- Butter

Instructions:
1. Mix a selected amount of minced meat with an egg or two and dash of cream. The goal is to make a smooth, but not loose, meat mixture. Season slightly. The cheese will add flavour. Mix well and let rest in the refrigerator.
2. When it is time to prepare your meal, use some baking paper and make one patty at a time from a tennis-size ball of meat mixture. Roll the ball into a roll and press flat.
3. Distribute cheese on the lengthwise half of the rectangle. With the help of the baking paper, fold the other half over to cover the cheese. Continue with the next roulade.
4. If I only fry 3–4 roulades, I finish them in the frying pan. Turn several times. When the cheese melts, they are finished. Add cream and cover. Simmer 15 minutes at low heat.
5. If I am going to fry many roulades, I brown them in the frying pan and put them in a pan in the oven. I bake them at medium heat until they are finished.

A large roulade (about 200 g) contains less than 1 g carbohydrates. Fat burning quotient: 1.1. This allows room for a little side dish. With a few tablespoons of cream sauce you have 2 g carbohydrates and a fat burning quotient of 1.4.

Well-seasoned minced meat patties

If you would like a kebab taste to your minced meat patties, add the following seasoning to the minced meat:
- Cumin
- Garlic
- Salt and Pepper

And supplement with, for example:
- Turmeric
- Coriander
- Oregano
- Ground bell pepper

Seared steak tartare

Steak tartare is one of my favourite dishes.
For four steak tartare you need:
- 600 g (21 oz) minced beef
- 1–2 tbs chopped onions
- 1–2 tbs chopped red beetroot
- 1–2 tbs chopped sour gherkins
- 1 tbs Dijon mustard
- Salt and pepper

Comments: I substitute gherkins for capers to avoid 5–6 g carbohydrates.

For the herbed butter you need:
- 2–3 tbs butter
- 1 finely chopped red onion
- 100 ml (3.5 fl oz) inexpensive red wine

Instructions:
1. Mix the steak tartare ingredients and set aside while you prepare the herb butter.

2. Sauté the onion in a little butter. Add wine and reduce. Pour into a cold bowl and cool. Add butter and mix, with a fork.

3. Shape four patties and sear them quickly in a hot frying pan, half a minute on each side. Put a dollop of herbed butter on each finished patty, and your meal is ready.

What about vegetables? They are in the steak tartare – which contains onions, beetroot, and gherkins. When you are in the 4+ group you can have half an avocado or a green salad in addition. A steak tartare provides 450–500 calories and 3 g carbohydrates, with a fat burning quotient of 1.0.

Gitsan's Swiss meatloaf

Here is an old recipe for Swiss meatloaf. Just before it is finished, brush it with a mixture of sugar-free tomato purée, soy sauce, and onion. You can drop this if you want to save a few tenths carbohydrates.

Ingredients:
- 500 g (1 lb 2 oz) minced beef
- 1 pkg bacon, fried crispy
- 2 eggs
- 400 g (14 oz) grated cheese
- 200 ml (7 fl oz) cream
- 1 chopped onion
- Salt, pepper, and French herbs

Mix and bake in the oven at 200 °C for 50–60 minutes.

If you slice this meatloaf into 6 portions, each slice provides 500 kcal, 2.2 g carbohydrates, and a fat burning quotient of 1.2. If you make it with minced pork, the fat burning quotient is 1.5.

About your green leaves

I often talk about supplementing with green leaves. They look appetising on a plate and allow your surroundings to think that you are eating healthy food. We aren't talking about large amounts, perhaps about 50 g (2 oz).

However, the kind of green leaves you choose matters. Here are the carbohydrate amounts for 50 g (2 oz) of common sorts:

- Endive, bitter, 0.4 g carbohydrates
- Frisée, bitter, 0.5 g carbohydrates
- Ruccola, peppery, 1.1 g carbohydrates
- Iceberg lettuce, mild, 1.1 g carbohydrates

Normally the bitter lettuces have a lower carbohydrate content, and the mild sorts are two to three times higher. Use the bitter sorts to garnish your plate!

Chicken salad with 2.2 g carbohydrates

If you don't want to, you don' t have to live on minced meat alone. You can make low carbohydrate salads; just avoid tomatoes and colourful peppers. Green bell pepper is an acceptable vegetable.

Instructions:

Mix 100 g (3.5 oz) fried chicken with a Florida salad. See the recipe on page 126.
Ready!
The salad contains about 500 kcal and only 2.2 g carbohydrates. Fat burning quotient: 1.4. Better food is hard to find!

Mervis' creamed spinach

Spinach is one of the few vegetables that has a natural place in the 8+ program. For some reason spinach is, one of the vegetables with the least carbohydrates. Asparagus is another one.

Melt frozen spinach in butter in a pan. Perhaps 100 g (3.5 oz) per person. Mix in a good quality cream cheese (with high fat content) and season to taste. Garlic adds extra zing to the dish.

This side dish is good with all fish and meats. Perfect when you are trying to get a child or an obstinate partner to eat vegetables.

Let's say you mix 400 g (14 oz) spinach with 100 g (3.5 oz) cream cheese. This gives 110 kcal and 2 g carbohydrates per 100 g portion. Fat burning quotient 1.5.

Courgette au gratin

Stuffed au gratin vegetables are delicious. In the 8+ group we normally stick to meat and green leaves. This is the basic food when you are trying to lose the first 4 stone (25 kg). However, there is actually one vegetable you can smuggle in now and then – courgette. A courgette with some of its flesh removed, filled with minced beef and baked in the oven, is low in carbohydrate. This dish contains only half of the courgette's original carbohydrates.

Other vegetables contain more carbohydrates. When you reach the 4+ group, you will have more to choose from. Bell pepper has one additional gram carbohydrate, aubergine and tomato have two more. Just now, there is no room for them in your diet, except for an extremely small portion.

Instructions:
1. Remove the flesh from a medium-sized courgette.

2. Fill with Wallenberg meat mixture.
3. Grate some good cheese on top.
4. Bake at 200 °C for about 30 minutes.

One portion of 300 g (10.5 oz) contains about 300 kcal and 3 g carbohydrates. Fat burning quotient: 1.5.

Nettle omelette

Nettles are green leaves, and green leaves are allowed in this program. In most cases, when I refer to green leaves it is as garnish, but now and then we can allow a supplement to the normal meat diet.

Nettles contain few carbohydrates and many healthy nutrients. They are some of our best vegetables. You won't find anything green in the grocery store with a comparable nutritional content. Provided you cut them down regularly, you can pick good nettle shoots long into the summer.

Nettles can be used in many dishes and are an excellent substitute for spinach. I prefer to sauté blanched nettles with bacon. I may add an egg and a few egg yolks. With a dash of cream it becomes a wonderful omelette. My omelette often contains more egg yolks than whole eggs and a good amount of cream. I need to hold the fat amount up to achieve satisfactory weight loss. If you function better on a more calorie-poor diet, use the whole egg and replace the cream with water.

Instructions:
Sauté as much bacon as you need. Perhaps half a pack per person. When the bacon is almost done, add a portion of blanched nettles and continue to sauté. After about a minute add a whole egg and three egg yolks. Follow with a dash of cream. Mix with a spatula to get a fluffy omelette. Season with black pepper and basil. Bacon adds enough salt.

I often share the omelette with my wife. There are about 400 calories per portion, with probably 3 g carbohydrates and a fat burning quotient of 2.

Carbohydrate-poor pork tenderloin

Stews are good, but they have a tendency to contain too many carbohydrates. I have a great pork tenderloin stew in the 4+ group, but it tips the scales at 6 g carbohydrates per portion. What can you do to adapt such a dish – or any dish for that matter – to the 8+ principles?

The answer is simple: Remove the carbohydrate-rich foods!

Suppose that you have a recipe that you like, but it contains too many carbohydrates. The objective is to remove or replace the source of carbohydrates without negatively affecting the original dish.

We can use my pork tenderloin stew for the 4+ group as an example. All the ingredients, with the exception of the pork tenderloin, contain carbohydrates. How can we halve the carbohydrates in this dish?

The original recipe, with a total of 6 g carbohydrates per portion, consists of:

- A pork tenderloin, about 500 g (1 lb 2 oz) (0 g carbohydrates)
- Fat, for example a mixture of olive oil and butter (0.1 g carbohydrates)
- 100 ml (3.5 fl oz) cream (3 g carbohydrates)
- 100 g (3.5 oz) crème fraîche (4 g carbohydrates)
- 50 g (2 oz) feta cheese (0.7 g carbohydrates)
- 1 large onion, I prefer red onion, (about 6 g carbohydrates)
- 1 bell pepper, about 100 g (3.5 oz) (3.1 g carbohydrates)
- 3 tbs capers, about 15 g (7.8 g carbohydrates)
- Season to taste

The capers have to go!

Who would believe it? A tablespoon of capers contains as many carbohydrates as cream, crème fraîche, and feta cheese all together! We drop the capers and substitute the sour taste with a tablespoon of apple cider vinegar (1 g carbohydrates). The cream stays. We reduce the amount of crème fraîche from 1 container to 2 tbs. Another 3 g carbohydrates disappears. If we use a small red onion, about 50 g (2 oz), we lose another 3 g carbohydrates.

When I enter this recipe into my nutritional program I get a total of 12 g carbohydrates for four portions. I add a few ounces of pork tenderloin to be sure that there is enough food. Here is the new recipe:

Pork tenderloin stew with 3 g carbohydrates per portion:

- 1 pork tenderloin, about 700 g, (1 lb 8 oz)
- 3 tbs fat, for example a mixture of olive oil and butter
- 100 ml (3.5 fl oz) cream
- 2 tbs crème fraîche
- 50 g (2 oz) feta cheese
- 1 small red onion, 50 g (2 oz)
- 1 bell pepper, about 100 g (3.5 oz)
- 1 tbs apple cider vinegar
- Seasoning to taste

The preparation is the same:

Brown the pork on both sides. Add onion and bell pepper, season, and fry together. When the vegetables are done, add cream and crème fraîche, add the vinegar, and crumble the feta into the pan. Cover and simmer.

If you use 700 g (1 lb 8 oz) pork tenderloin, you will have about two pounds of casserole with a total of 1800 kcal. Divided into four portions, we are just at the limit of 3 g carbohydrates per portion. Fat burning quotient: 0.7.

Minute steak stuffed with cheese

I probably ate about 16 stone (100 kg) of minute steak stuffed with cheese while I was losing weight. There are many reasons – one is that I love this dish, another is that it is perfect hiking and travel food.

Ingredients:
Minute steaks, many of them
Tasty cheese
Dijon mustard
Fat and seasoning

Instructions:
1. Put some minute steaks on a cutting board. Season them now or later during frying.
2. Place some pieces of cheese on half of each steak.
3. Spread a little mustard on the cheese.
4. Fold the other half of the steak over the cheese, not quite even with the edge of the lower half so that the steak will stick together more easily.
5. Fry the steak until the cheese starts to melt. If you have many to fry up, it is smart to brown them on both sides and let them bake in the oven until they are done.

I usually fry many minute steaks, eat a few for dinner and store the rest until needed. They are almost better cold.

One 120 g (4.5 oz) fried, stuffed minute steak contains 240 kcal and only 0.9 g carbohydrates. Fat burning quotient 0.6. If you eat two minute steaks, you have room for a few green leaves.

Another alternative is to stuff with blue cheese. Then you drop the mustard.

Salmon pâté with few carbohydrates

Salmon pâté is good and something you don't have to say no to in the 8+ group. You can easily make salmon pâté without flour, just like you can make an omelette without flour.

I found a recipe online. It was based on egg, cottage cheese, cream, and cold salmon. Delicious! The cottage cheese is supposed to be strained but when I opened carton, I discovered that it was only a quarter full. What to do? I usually make scrambled eggs and omelettes with mayonnaise, so my first impulse was to do the same here.

My first try went like this:

- 300–400 g (10.5–14 lb) salmon. I combined one part cold smoked salmon with two parts uncooked salmon fillet.
- 300 ml (10.5 fl oz) cream
- 200 g (7 oz) drained cottage cheese. Press out the liquid or let it drain out on its own.
- 4 eggs
- 100 ml (3.5 fl oz) mayonnaise
- A good amount of pepper and enough salt
- Dill if you want; I usually drop it

Combine the ingredients, put the mixture in a casserole, and bake at 200 °C. After about 50 minutes the pâté should have a nice colour. To be sure if it's done, I let it stand a while longer in the oven, but that was probably not necessary. The result was perfect.

I have since made this pâté several times with slightly different ingredients. I have tried the original recipe with 500 g (18 oz) cottage cheese and no mayonnaise, but I prefer the taste of the version with mayonnaise. This version has more calories, but the fat burning quotient is better. Both versions are excellent.

A 200 g (7 oz) portion of salmon pâté provides about 570 kcal and 2.7 g carbohydrates. This is the mayonnaise version. The fat burning quotient is 2.0. If you eat your portion with 2 tbs melted butter, you have 780 kcal and a fat burning quotient of 3.

Minute steak with stroganoff flavour

I am really fond of beef stroganoff – but, unfortunately, several of the ingredients contain too many carbohydrates. The tomato purée is worst, but sugar-free tomato purée is available. Even the cream and the freshly squeezed lemon juice contain more carbohydrates than you would think.

I have reduced the carbohydrate totals for my beef stroganoff recipe to make a beef stew that has at least a hint of stroganoff flavour.

1. Sauté half an onion in a few tablespoons of butter. Remove the onion, but keep the butter!
2. Add more butter and fry strips of minute steak in the same pan. 300–400 g (10.5 – 14 oz) is enough for two people. Add salt, pepper and some stock.
3. Flavour with
   - 1 tbs sugar-free tomato purée
   - 1 tbs crème fraîche
   - 1 tsp lemon juice
   - 1 tsp Dijon mustard
4. Round off the taste with 500 ml (around 1 pint) cream

This makes two portions with less than 3 g carbohydrates per portion. 500 calories per portion if you count calories, and a fat burning quotient of 0.8.

PS. This is not a real beef stroganoff, just a great approximation of one. When you reach the 4+ group you can add more cream and more tomato purée. And you can let the onion stay in the pan! If you are waiting for something good, perhaps you are waiting for a real beef stroganoff …

Steak anno 1926

Do you remember how an old-fashioned steak with onions tasted? I read old cookbooks for fun and found a typical recipe in *Husmoderns kokbok* (The Housewife's cookbook), published in 1926.

Ingredients:
- Steak
- Red onion
- Butter
- Salt and white pepper
- Boiling water

Instructions:
Cut the meat into 3 cm thick slices and pound it on both sides with a kitchen mallet. Salt and pepper.

Brown the meat in the butter in a hot pan. One minute on each side is enough.

Put the meat on a warm plate and brown the onions in the same pan. Put the golden brown onions on the plate with the steak.

Deglaze the pan with boiling water, mix, and pour over the steak.

Sometimes I make a steak like this, mostly for the fun of it. Then I use a herb butter, even though it is not traditional to do so.

A 150 g (5.5 oz) piece of fried steak with a little portion of fried onions contains less than 300 kcal and less than 3 g carbohydrates. Fat burning quotient: 0.2. Since it is the protein that reduces the fat burning quotient, there is no a problem. We can tolerate 40 g protein in a meal. With a dollop of herb butter you can raise the fat burning quotient to 0.6.

Josefine's chicken liver

I got this recipe from a Norwegian friend. It is a remarkably simple recipe that is excellent GI-Zero! food.

Ingredients:
- 300 g (10.5 oz) chicken liver
- 3 tbs butter
- 2 tbs olive oil
- 150 g (5.5 oz) frozen spinach
- 200 ml (7 fl oz) cream
- Seasoning to taste

Instructions:
1. Cut the liver into pieces and sauté it in a mixture of butter and olive oil. At medium heat this takes about 10 minutes.
2. Add spinach and cream. Simmer for 4–5 minutes.
3. Season to taste.

The whole recipe provides about 1900 kcal and 12 g carbohydrates. Fat burning quotient: 1.36. In the 8+ group you can eat a fourth of the recipe. If you primarily eat the chicken livers you can eat a little more. Other groups can eat the whole portion.

Margareta's chicken liver mousse

We should eat liver at least once a week. It provides us with a surplus of vitamins and minerals. However, shop-bought liver pâté contains many questionable ingredients. Here is a simple recipe that takes no time to prepare:

- 400 g (14 oz) chicken liver
- 100–200 g (3.5 – 7 oz) butter
- 200 ml (7 fl oz) cream
- Salt and seasonings to taste

Sauté the chicken liver in lots of butter until it is done (this goes faster if you cut the liver into smaller pieces). Season with salt and pepper, add other seasoning according to your preferences (I use some herbs and garlic).

Mix the liver in a food processor with the cream and a little extra butter, perhaps also more seasoning. Pour the mixture into a tray that has a lid. It has a loose consistency, but don't worry. The pâté will stiffen in the refrigerator.

The original recipe makes a pâté with a normal liver pâté consistency, without chemical additives. Perfect in all situations where you want to serve a pâté.

Divided into 4 portions, there are 500–600 kcal per portion, depending on the amount of butter, 2.4 g carbohydrates and a fat burning quotient of over 2.

There is nothing to stop you from expanding the pâté a little, but then you end up with a dish for the 4+ group. Some anchovies add taste, but also extra carbohydrates. A little crispy bacon and a chopped onion are other possibilities. Or a portion of sautéed mushrooms. A pâté with these ingredients will contain 5 g carbohydrates per portion and a fat burning quotient of 2. These ingredients will also result in a looser and more grainy consistency.

Classic casserole from leftovers

You will find many casseroles in old cookbooks. They are easy to make, can be made from almost anything, and are the perfect way to use leftovers.

You need three basic *ingredients:* cheese, cream, and meat. You can also use eggs if you want to, but it isn't necessary.

In addition, you can use the leftovers you have in your refrigerator. I have made casseroles with lamb, chicken, ham, smoked herring, cold-smoked salmon, and anything else.

Instructions:

Start with the leftover meats and add roughly equal parts of cheese and cream. If you have 400 g (14 oz) fish, add 300–400 g (10.5 – 14 oz) chopped cheese and 400 ml (14 fl oz) cream. Or something like that. Then everything goes into the oven at about 200 °C until it looks done. Now that wasn't so difficult, was it?

I found this combination on the internet:

- 600 g (21 oz) smoked ham
- 400 g (14 oz) cheese
- 500 ml (just under a pint) cream

I had some smoked ham at home, so I tried it. I ran the cheese and ham through the food processor, put the mixture in a tray, added the cream, and put it in the oven. I used some flavourful cheese, and smoked ham is tasty on its own, so I didn't season the dish. It turned out delicious.

This combination makes a casserole with 4000 kcal and 20 g carbohydrates. I ate half and felt like a python that had swallowed a pig. I was full for ten hours.

If you divide the casserole into 8 portions, each will be 500 kcal and 2.6 g carbohydrates. Fat burning quotient: 1.3.

Ground pike is delicious

I have a wonderful recipe on page 142. I mix pike and salmon, but you can make it with just pike. The recipe is for the 4+ program, but if the ground pike is eaten with melted butter, it works for the 8+ group as well.

Swiss schnitzel can be carbohydrate-free

Do you know what a Swiss schnitzel is? It is a real treat. Like a wiener schnitzel, but with cheese and ham in the centre. It is absolutely great if you use real veal, but you can apply the principle to other meats too.

The problem with schnitzel is in the breadcrumbs. If you really breadcrumb the meat on both sides, you can easily come up to 10 g carbohydrates per portion. When I calculated this schnitzel, I came up with a total of 1.1 g! The solution is to breadcrumb with ground, deep-fried bacon rinds.

Ingredients:
- Two thick slices of veal, or another meat. Tell your butcher what you are going to do with them; that is about the only place you can get cuts like this.
- A thick slice of smoked ham, about the same size as the veal slices.
- Cheese.
- Bacon rinds – but be sure that they really are made of pork!
- 1 egg
- Salt and pepper

Instructions:
Press or pound the pieces of veal until they are the same size, then apply salt and pepper.

Cover one slice first with cheese, then with ham. Cover the ham with cheese as well.

Put the second slice of veal on top and make sure the stack is a nice shape.

Breadcrumb as you usually do, but use ground, deep-fried bacon rinds instead of flour. I usually brush with beaten egg and turn the schnitzel in the bacon rinds several times.

Fry in butter until the cheese melts.

Deglaze the pan to make a sauce. Anchovies and some seasoning are a good addition.

If you divide the schnitzel into 4 pieces, each piece will have 300 kcal and 0.5 g carbohydrates. You have room for some green leaves. Schnitzel also tastes good cold and is great hiking food. One piece is a snack, two pieces are a dinner. Fat burning quotient: 0.53.

Meat soup is good food

Boil the meat together with vegetables of your choice. Eat the meat and leave the vegetables!

Meat soups and stews can easily be made the day before so the flavour has a opportunity to develop. Use meat from the front part of the animal, including bone, and consider yourself lucky if the pieces are fat. Season to taste. Let the soup clear at a low heat.

Boiled beef has a fat burning quotient of 0.7. Pork has 1.2. If you boil equal parts beef and pork together, you have a fat burning quotient of 0.9. A portion of 200 g (7 oz) has 600 kcal and no carbohydrates.

Dill meat

A few hours ago I found two pounds of pork ribs in the refrigerator. I usually brush ribs with a mixture of oil, Dijon mustard, and seasoning, and bake them in the oven. Instead, I decided to boil them so that I could make dill meat. I almost always make dill meat with lamb, sometimes with veal, but I have never made it from pork before.

Instructions:

1. I folded the ribs and pushed them into a pot. Added water, salt, and 10–12 white pepper corns, plus a bouillon cube. I couldn't find any bay leaves.
2. I chopped an onion and a carrot and put it in the pot.

Only to add taste! Then I set the pot on the stove at a low heat and went up to my office to continue writing this book. An hour and a half later, the meat was done.

3. It was time to make a sauce. I sieved some of the stock into a pan and seasoned with lemon juice and dill. On low heat I mixed in two egg yolks and some cream. Then I stirred until the sauce had a nice consistency.

4. After that I ate a portion to taste the recipe. It tasted great, so I ate another portion.

That was twenty minutes ago, and I can still feel the warm, good feeling spreading through my body. This was an excellent variation on pork ribs!

A normal portion will likely consist of 150 g (5.5 oz) meat plus sauce (I ate twice that!). This provides 450 kcal and only 1 g carbohydrate. Fat burning quotient: 0.7. If you keep the cooked vegetables, remember that 50 g (1.7 oz) cooked onions is 3 g carbohydrates and 50 g (1.7 oz) carrots is 4.6 g carbohydrates! No room for them within your limit of 3 g per meal. But if you accidentally eat a bit of onion, no serious damage is done.

Airam's chicken with Boursin sauce

I found this chicken recipe on Airam's internet food blog. I often make recipes like this myself. I haven't tried this one but I am going to one day soon.

Instructions:

1. Brown a chicken, preferably in flavourful fat. Bacon grease is good. Season.

2. Put the chicken into an oven pan. Add garlic and perhaps a few vegetables. Pour pan drippings over. Bake at 200 °C for 40 minutes.

3. Remove chicken and set aside.

4. Pour pan drippings into a saucepan and add a Boursin cheese with pepper flavour.
5. Melt the cheese while stirring.
6. Add 100-200 ml (3.5–7 fl oz) cream and reduce to the desired consistency.
7. Season to taste.

A portion of chicken plus sauce provides 600 kcal and less than 2 g carbohydrates. Fat burning quotient: 1.3. You have room for a sautéed bell pepper without exceeding your limit of 3 g.

Meat with sheep's milk cheese au gratin

Here comes one of my favourite recipes. I use it when I want to make a new dish, based on leftover chicken, pork loin, or lamb. Previous generations were experts at making something new from whatever they had at hand. That art is well worth rediscovering!

I take what I have out of the refrigerator, leftovers of a lamb roast or yesterday's pork loin stew. Or I fry up something, pork roast or chicken fillets. I can combine beef, pork, chicken, or lamb – don't be limited by conventions!

For this dish you need two ingredients:
– Meat, about 150–200 g (5.5 oz – 7 oz) per person
– Sheep's milk cheese for for au gratin sauce

Sheep's milk cheese sauce:
– 100 ml (3.5 fl oz) cream
– 100 ml (3.5 fl oz) crème fraîche (I actually prefer to use 200 ml (7 fl oz), but that adds too many carbohydrates for the 8+ group)
– 100 g (3.5 oz) sheep's milk cheese
– 1–2 garlic cloves
– Salt and pepper

Instructions:
1. Pre-heat the oven to 200 °C.
2. Put the meat in an oven-proof baking tray.
3. Mash the cheese and mix it with the crème fraîche and cream. Add crushed garlic. Pour the sauce over the meat.
4. Bake for 10–15 minutes.

One portion contains about 300 kcal and 2.6 g carbohydrates. Fat burning quotient: 0.5. You have room to decorate with some green leaves.

Parboiled salmon with creamed nettles

I created this dish a few days ago. We had some fresh salmon in the refrigerator, and as usual, our yard was full of nettles. This should set the stage for a low carbohydrate dish! It turned out really well, and the dish is perfect for the 8+ group.

Instructions:
1. Gather a good portion of nettles. I wear a thick glove on my left hand, grab the nettle and cut it so that I have a few leaves as well. It is better to take only the tops, but the harvesting will take you twice as long.
2. Rinse the nettles and blanch them in fresh water with a bouillon cube.
3. Drain off the water, but save it for stock. Sauté the nettles in butter. Add a dash of cream and reduce.
4. Parboil the salmon in a little water with butter, lemon juice, and seasoning. Bring to a boil, turn off, and cover. A few minutes later the fish is ready.
5. Eat and enjoy.

200 g (7 oz) salmon together with a portion of creamed nettles contains 700 kcal and 2 g carbohydrates. Fat burning quotient: 1.1. This is healthy food!

Alternatively you can eat your salmon with the Mervis' creamed spinach recipe on page 99. With 150 g (5.5 oz) creamed spinach you have 640 g kcal, barely 3 g carbohydrates, and a fat burning quotient of 0.8.

Low carbohydrate fish soup

Fish soup is easy to make and good to eat. In this carbohydrate-stingy group we use two parts fish and one part vegetables. This gives 3 g carbohydrates per portion and we don't have to do any more maths. The only thing that we have to remember is not to eat root vegetables. We can put a few carrots and a parsnip in, but only for the sake of taste. Remove these vegetables before you eat the soup (a small carrot contains 6 g carbohydrates; a large one can contain 20!).

Instructions:

I sauté a pound of mixed vegetables in some tablespoons of olive oil. Perhaps a shallot, broccoli, a yellow onion, and a few yellow and/or red peppers. I use whatever I have available. I cut the shallot into thin slices, the rest I chop. Maybe a chopped garlic clove as well. A small chopped tomato will add a nice colour. Otherwise saffron is a classic colour and taste addition to fish soups, but don't use too much!

I season with salt and pepper and add about a litre of fish stock. Perhaps some dry white wine too. Simmer.

When it is almost time to eat, add two pounds of fish cut into pieces. Bring the soup to a boil. I usually use a mixture of salmon and white fish. When the soup has boiled for a few minutes, turn off the heat, and season to taste. In my case, I often add ground bell pepper, a little cayenne pepper, and perhaps a drop of lemon juice.

A bowl of soup contains 260 kcal and 3 g carbohydrates. Fat burning quotient: 0.7.

Airam's smörgåstårta

Let's end this chapter with a wonderful Swedish speciality. Up until now there has been a lot of meat, because a diet rich in meat is the simplest way to start a successful journey to health. However, once in a while it can be nice to eat something completely different. Here is a well-known deviation from the animal category.

This dish includes nothing dangerous; the only problem is that it is so delectable that it can weaken our will and tempt us to abandon our journey! Regard it as an extravagance, a reward to enjoy when we have everything under control. Notice the following: we reward ourselves when everything is going well, but our reward is still good food!

When we begin to feel that our current diet is boring, or when we have reached a weight loss plateau, we must still stick to the program. Whether we have the willpower to see it through or not is the difference between success and failure!

Airam has a great food blog on the internet. She is an excellent cook, but normally she works as a nurse. She creates, photographs, and presents one superb recipe after another. I got permission to borrow some special treats from her, and this *smörgåstårta* was my first choice. A large slice of inviting *smörgåstårta* only contains 3 g carbohydrates! What do you think of that?

To make the bread:

Mix at least 8 eggs with 100 ml (3.5 fl oz) cream. Let the mixture bake (on baking paper in an oven pan) at 225 °C. Try to make a bread with straight edges.

When the surface is dry, turn the bread, and bake the

other side. You can make an excellent roll out of this. I have done it!

But this is Airam's *smörgåstårta* we are going to make. Cool the bread and divide it into 4 pieces. Save the nicest piece for the top. Then we start to load up with luscious fillings.

You can fill your *smörgåstårta* with whatever you want, but this is what Airam does:
– Bottom filling: an egg cream made of chopped, hard-boiled eggs mixed with butter.
– Layer 2: Shrimp salad with dill.
– Layer 3: A sauce of crème fraîche, mayonnaise, chopped shrimp, catfish caviar, and smoked salmon strips.

Put the top piece on and cover the whole *smörgåstårta* with a mixture of crème fraîche and mayonnaise. Garnish with cucumber slices around the sides.

And now comes the crowning glory:
A wreath of crispy lettuce and hardboiled egg slices. Lots of shrimp. Dollops of caviar. Parsley and dill. A few tomato wedges.

If you are really bold, you can decorate with things that you can't eat, like grapes. But remember that there is a difference between beauty and food!

Refrigerate for a few hours to let the taste develop. Your guests will be surprised at how luxuriously you can eat while you are losing weight!

In the 8+ group you can eat one 250 g (9 oz) slice. From which you will get about 600 kcal and 3 g carbohydrates. Fat burning quotient: 2.0.

A summary
of the 4+ program

The plate model for the 4+ group:

Two parts animal foods and one part vegetable. Only vegetables that grow above ground are permitted. Take care with tomatoes. Carbohydrate limit: 6 g per meal, 18 g carbohydrates per day.

This is the normal GI-Zero! program for those who have halved the amount they're overweight with the help of recipes in the 8+ group. Here we try to add a few more grams of carbohydrates with each meal. At this point, your body's fat metabolism is turned on, and a few additional carbohydrates in an otherwise fat and animal-based diet shouldn't cause problems.

This is also the group for those who don't have to deal with the problem of being extremely overweight. If you weigh 3 to 4 stone (19–25 kg) too much, you can start in this group. You will recover your good health in just a few months – even if you don't feel sick today. You will quickly discover what good health really feels like. In addition, you will achieve gradual weight loss.

Evaluate your progress after three months, not after three weeks. If you are burning fat at a reasonable rate, continue the program. If you are losing more than two pounds a week, you should go on to the 2+ program. The risk of loose skin is not so great in this group, so you can also choose to stay in the 4+ group until you have reached your weight loss goal.

You are probably less carbohydrate-sensitive than those in the 8+ group. This means that you should eat fat and meat as basic foods, and vegetables as supplements. Only vegetables that grow above ground are permitted, and even these only in small amounts. Measured in energy percent, you can consume 25–30 percent protein, 65–70 percent fat, and about 5 percent carbohydrate.

In the 4+ group you can use all the recipes in the 8+ group and add an approved side dish. Florida salad, creamed spinach or half an avocado with lemon juice is good with almost everything. A few of my frittatas can also be recommended as side dishes.

A normal day on 4+

What can you eat in the 4+ group? You can eat whatever you want! Provided, of course, that you use the recipes that are provided for this group and the 8+ group. As you will soon discover, the recipes in this group are similar to the 8+ group. However, the three extra grams of carbohydrates per meal actually make a big difference. With few exceptions, in the 8+ group you were only allowed to garnish your meat or fish with green leaves. In the 4+ group, you can add modest amounts of vegetables to almost every meal, or a large amount to a special meal.

You should be aware of the fact that you can always save carbohydrates during the day, and then eat a solid portion of greens for dinner. Even if you saved all the carbohydrates allowed in one day and consumed them in a single meal, 18 g isn't enough to cause a significant rise in blood sugar levels. Your metabolism of fat will continue as planned.

You can also combine the recipes in this group as you wish. It is possible to create many different menus. I can't tell you what to eat, that depends on your personal tastes and the life you lead. All combinations of the approved recipes are allowed.

Breakfast

Quick shrimp and avocado salad or bacon omelette. See the section on breakfast on pages 35 and 38. (When you really get going on this diet, a few cold minute steaks stuffed with cheese will give you an excellent start to the day, but that may be difficult for you to believe just yet!).

Lunch (when you are hungry, not just because it is noon)

Why not have meat patties with feta cheese and coleslaw? This is a good and nutritional combination. You can warm up the meat patties quickly and you have a lot of coleslaw in the refrigerator.

I expect you to have ready-to-eat food in your refrigerator. If you make double portions for dinner, you always have access to nutritional fast food! Of course this is if you eat at home. If you eat at work, take a packed lunch; that is your best solution. Eating lunch out is a big gamble. Then you have to take what you get. Buffets are good. It is easy to put together a good meal. Kebab salad without bread is a possibility. In a pinch, you can buy two open-face shrimp sandwiches and not eat the bread.

The recipe for meat patties is on page 92, coleslaw on page 133. 150 g (5.5 oz) meat patties, some tablespoons of sauce, and a small portion of coleslaw provide 600 kcal and 5.7 g carbohydrates. Fat burning quotient: 1.8!

Dinner

If you look at the recipes in this chapter, you will find salmon pâté with spinach. This is the same pâté recipe that you find in the 8+ group on page 104. But now you can add an additional 3 g carbohydrates. For example, you can put sautéed spinach in the bottom of the tray and then add the rest of the ingredients. Nutritious and delicious.

With 200 g (7 oz) sautéed spinach, 200 g (7 oz) salmon, and 2 tbs melted butter you have 900 kcal and about 6 g carbohydrates. Fat burning quotient: 2.3.

Comments

These are a few quick suggestions. You can combine any of the recipes in this group as you please. If you want to eat a traditional breakfast, select one or two of my recipes from the section on breakfast. Then the day starts on schedule. After that, you can plough through the next chapter. When you have found 5–6 favourite recipes, you have a good foundation.

After you have practised this diet for a time, the principles become second nature. Then you can start to explore food articles in the newspaper and cookbooks. Often it takes no more than dropping the side dishes and replacing them with some from the program. Rice and root vegetables do not belong in THE SCANDINAVIAN DIET, while creamed spinach, Florida salad, and coleslaw are not a problem.

Recipes for 4+

Luxurious minced beef with asparagus and mashed broccoli

If you have flicked through the recipes for the 8+ group, you may have noticed the recipe for Wallenberg's fakir steak. It is a delicious recipe, but it looks a little forlorn on a plate all by itself. Now that you have reached the 4+ group, you have the opportunity to add some tasty side dishes.

A true Wallenberg is served with mashed potatoes and green peas. I give you permission to eat a small portion of mashed broccoli and a few spears of asparagus! This is not a bad alternative. When you reach the 2+ group you can allow yourself more mashed broccoli.

Instructions:

Mix the ingredients for the Wallenberg's fakir steak and put aside while you prepare the side dishes.

Making mashed broccoli is easy. Cook the broccoli in salted water with a slice of butter until tender. Drain and mash the broccoli with butter and cream. 100 g (3.5 oz) mashed broccoli contains 100 kcal and 3.5 g carbohydrates (alternatively you can use my recipe for mashed vegetables).

If you choose asparagus, it is even simpler. Open the tin! The tinned kind is ready in the blink of an eye and is low in carbohydrates. Fresh asparagus must boil for about 30 minutes. Tinned asparagus takes no more than 4–5 minutes to cook.

A Wallenberg (500 g, 17.5 oz) with 100 g (3.5 oz) mashed broccoli and a few asparagus spears provides 600 kcal and a total of 5.5 g carbohydrates. Fat burning quotient: 1.8!

My mashed vegetables

We don't eat mashed potatoes with GI-Zero!, but once in a while I would really like some. When I eat Wallenbergs, I often accompany them with asparagus and mashed broccoli, butter, and cream. Sometimes I include cauliflower or an avocado. You can mash most vegetables.

Instructions:

I cook the vegetables in lightly salted water until tender. I use broccoli as a base, but many use cauliflower instead. Drain off the water and let the vegetables steam. Add butter and cream. Mash with a potato masher (very easy to clean).

Nutmeg is a good seasoning for all kinds of mash. Sometimes I mix in an avocado for a milder taste. Coconut milk is also wonderful to mix in, but use the thick part, not the thin. You don't want it be a soup.

With soup as first course

One day, I cooked some broccoli in water, drained off the water, and added avocado and coconut milk. Unfortunately I dumped the whole tin in the pan, and the mixture became very runny. I let it simmer for a while and then sieved the broth over into a soup bowl. Salt, pepper, a lot of Indian seasoning, and some cayenne pepper added taste. My teenager ate this accidental soup with great gusto.

I then prepared a mash of the vegetables and the remaining broth, and ate it with a piece of home-made pâté. Excellent.

Cooked broccoli and cauliflower contain 3 g carbohydrates per 100 g (3.5 oz). Avocado contains a little more, coconut milk less.

When I calculated a portion of mashed vegetables, they contained 3.25 g carbohydrates per 100 g (3.5 oz) regardless of whether they were mixed with butter and cream or coconut milk. If you use coconut milk the fat burning quotient is 1.4; with butter and cream it is 2.15. Why is it higher with butter and cream? Because the amount of fat increases!

Mervis' luxurious creamed spinach

Creamed spinach is easy. You can make it with cream cheese or cream. Flour is never necessary.

Instructions:
Using 400 g (14 oz) spinach, 200 ml (7 fl oz) cream, and a handful of walnuts, you get a fatty and luxurious mixture. Great for those of us who need to keep the fat percent high. Creamed spinach contains about 230 kcal and 3–4 g carbohydrates per 100 g (3.5 oz). More than half of these carbohydrates comes from the walnuts! Decide yourself whether or not you have room for them. Fat burning quotient: 2.7.

Without the walnuts, you have 2 g carbohydrates per 100 g (3.5 oz) creamed spinach. The energy amount drops to 160 kcal, and the fat burning quotient rises to 3.

If you need to watch your calorie intake, 100 ml (3.5 fl oz) cream is enough for 400 g (14 oz) sautéed spinach. Then you have 125 kcal and less than 2 g carbohydrates per portion. Fat burning quotient: 2.1.

You can adjust your recipes back and forth according to your need. You will quickly discover what works best for you. Those who weigh 4 stone (25 kg) too much need a fat-rich diet. Occasionally there are people who achieve better results by reducing the fat percent and letting the protein stand for a higher percent of the energy intake. Carbohydrates must always stay at low levels.

Beef stroganoff

When I prepare beef stroganoff, I use high quality, tender meat, preferably sirloin from a country with grass grazing animals. Brazil, Argentina, New Zealand, and Ireland have good meats. Despite the long transport they are better products than the industrially produced meats we often get in Europe.

Sugar-free tomato purée is available; use it instead of the sugared varieties. You save a few grams of carbohydrates. This recipe serves two.

Instructions:
1. Chop a medium-sized onion and fry carefully in a few tablespoons of butter until transparant. Remove the onion, keep only half, or there will be too many carbohydrates.
2. Add butter, increase the heat, and fry beef strips quickly in the same pan. 300–400 g (10.5 – 14 oz) is enough for two people. Turn down the heat and add the sautéed onions. Season with salt and pepper.
3. Add 100 ml (3.5 fl oz) cream and mix. Then add the following:
   – 2 tbs sugar-free tomato purée
   – 100 g (3.5 oz) crème fraîche
   – 100 ml (3.5 fl oz) dry white wine, or 1 tsp lemon juice
   – 1 tsp Dijon mustard
4. Cover and simmer.

This makes two good portions. Served on some green leaves, it is barely 700 kcal per portion, with about 6 g carbohydrates and a fat burning quotient of 1.25.

P.S.: When you are in the 2+ group, you can add more cream and onions. Or you can have a good green salad or half an avocado.

Cheese-stuffed minute steak with side dishes

Stuffing meat with cheese and frying until the cheese melts is a fantastic way to create delicious meals. You can use this principle with all thin slices of fresh meat. I have tried pork and fish too; it all works. If it is possible to fold the meat, more of the cheese stays inside the "package".

I really enjoy cheese-stuffed minute steak. You can stuff them with hard cheeses and mustard, or blue cheese. It all tastes good.

A 120 g (4.5 oz) fried, stuffed minute steak contains about 240 kcal and only 0.9 g carbohydrates. Fat burning quotient: 0.6. If you eat two steaks you can choose a side dish with 3–4 g carbohydrates. A small portion of coleslaw or a large portion of creamed spinach are good alternatives.

Two fried cheese steaks with a small portion of coleslaw provide 600 kcal, with 5.6 g carbohydrates, and a fat burning quotient of 0.73. If you choose creamed spinach instead, you can eat twice as much without increasing the carbohydrate content.

Florida salad

Carin's mother brought this recipe back with her from Florida.

Ingredients:
1. 1–2 pkg bacon
2. 1 small head of cauliflower
3. 1 tube mayonnaise
4. 1 head of iceberg lettuce

Instructions:
Chop the cauliflower into tiny pieces; it is going to be eaten raw. Chop the bacon and fry it. Mix the cauliflower, bacon, mayonnaise, and lettuce.

This salad goes will with almost anything, especially grilled meats. Lots of people have trouble determining what the salad contains, but everyone likes it. I use it as an alternative to coleslaw. A 100 g (3.5 oz) portion contains 2.5 g carbohydrates. Fat burning quotient: 2.5.

Puréed fish soup with side dishes

Fish soup is good and can be made without a recipe. You need fish, vegetables, and fish stock. And your preferred seasoning. I have a simple recipe on page 115. The soup contains only 3 g carbohydrates per portion, which is the limit in the 8+ group. In the 4+ group you can add some cream, and then purée with a hand-held immersion blender or food processor.

Instructions:
1. Prepare the soup according to my basic recipe. Use twice as much fish as vegetables. Sauté the vegetables in oil until transparent, add fish stock and fish. It can't get any simpler. So far you have just followed the recipe.
2. Add cream according to taste and purée the soup.
3. Prepare side dishes of choice.

4. Heat the soup, sprinkle with finely chopped parsley, and serve.

You have room for some good side dishes, like baked cheese crisps, cheese balls, or perhaps some cheese macaroons. Cheese balls you make from grated cheese and crème fraîche. Season with cayenne pepper. Cheese macaroons are simply cheese melted on baking paper in the oven.

A bowl of puréed fish soup without side dishes contains 340 kcal and 4 g carbohydrates. Fat burning quotient: 1.0. If you accompany the soup with 2 baked cheese crisps, 3 cheese meringues, or a cheese ball you add 200 kcal and 1–2 g carbohydrates, depending on the type of cheese.

How I prepare pork tenderloin (and all other tenderloins)

It is easy to prepare pork tenderloin; in fact, it is nearly impossible to fail. I usually prepare it in my large frying pan and let it simmer under a lid. You have a lot of freedom with regard to ingredients, but this is how I do it:

1. 1 pork tenderloin
2. Fat, a mixture of olive oil and butter
3. 100 ml (3.5 fl oz) cream
4. 100 g (3.5 oz) crème fraîche
5. A piece of feta cheese
6. A large onion, I prefer a red onion
7. A bell pepper
8. A few tsp capers
9. Seasoning of choice

Most of these ingredients can be replaced by others. If I use beef tenderloin, I drop the bell pepper and add a few tablespoons of sugar-free tomato purée, half a tablespoon of Dijon Mustard, and a dash of lemon juice. Presto, a beef stroganoff!

Instructions:
Cut the pork loin in thin slices and brown them on both sides. Add onion and bell pepper, season, and fry. When the vegetables are tender, add the cream and crème fraîche, add the capers and crumble feta cheese over everything. Cover and simmer.

If you use 500 g (17.5 oz) pork loin, there will be two pounds including sauce and vegetables, altogether 1800 kcal and 24 g carbohydrates. Your serving can equal a quarter of the dish if you want to keep within the limits of 6 g carbohydrates. Fat burning quotient: 0.94.

How I prepare ratatouille

I never follow a recipe when I make food; I just use what I have at hand. Ratatouille is a French mixed vegetable dish that is well-suited for spontaneous food preparation. If you belong to the 4+ group you can allow yourself a ratatouille now and then, while those in the 2+ group can eat it every day.

Ingredients:
1. Fat, for example coconut and olive oil
2. Yellow onion, a large amount
3. Bell peppers in different colours
4. Garlic
5. Chilli paste or chillies
6. Lemon
7. Salt and seasoning, for example ground bell pepper, cayenne pepper, coriander, cumin. A cube of chicken bouil-

lon is a good idea. Sometimes I use sugar-free tomato purée. (NB! Not ketchup!)

Supplement with other ingredients that you have in the house, for example:

1. Courgette
2. Tomatoes, in moderation
3. Shallots
4. Or anything else that grows above ground

Instructions:

Start by lightly sautéing the coarsely-chopped onion in the oil. When it is transparent, add the courgette and bell pepper, also coarsely chopped. Add chopped garlic cloves, salt and pepper. I use medium heat, so the vegetables are barely tender. Then I add the remaining vegetables, plus a tin of chopped tomatoes. I like to add a tablespoon of chilli paste, but you might find that a teaspoon is enough? Finally I add some lemon juice to round off.

After 15 minutes you can eat the ratatouille, but I usually let it simmer for an hour. All according to your taste.

The nutritional content depends on the ingredients that you use. My ratatouille has a fat burning quotient of 0.6, and that is fine. But the carbohydrate total is quite high. With this recipe you have a 100 g (3.5 oz) mixture of vegetables that contain about 5 g carbohydrates. With a piece of meat and a bit of butter you reach the limit of 6 g carbohydrates per meal. However, if you have consumed fewer carbohydrates in your other meals, you can have 250 g (8.5 oz) ratatouille for dinner. You decide.

Seared steak tartare with side dishes

I like steak tartare, but for safety's sake I sear it first. You will find a low carbohydrate recipe on page 96. The only difference from the restaurant varieties is that I use gherkins instead of capers. Capers actually taste better in a steak tartare, but these tasty buds are high in carbohydrates.

Follow the previously mentioned recipe and supplement with 3 g carbohydrates if you wish. That corresponds to half an avocado or some lettuce. There is also room for a few tablespoons of a low carbohydrate dressing.

One steak with accompaniments provides 650 kcal, 6 g carbohydrates, and has a fat burning quotient of 1.3.

Mutton and cabbage stew ("fårikål")

"Fårikål" is classic peasant food, with the advantage that the dish is prepared in one pot. If you have a large enough pot, you can make ten or twenty servings at once. It is no more trouble than making one dinner. This is perfect food to have in the freezer. Inexpensive too!

The problem that confronts us when we look up this dish in a cookbook, is that the recipe calls for large amounts of cabbage. Cabbage contains 4 g carbohydrates per 100 g (3.5 oz) and should be eaten with moderation.

Ingredients:
1. At least 1 kg (2 lb 3 oz) lamb, shoulder or shanks are good
2. Some tablespoons of butter to brown the meat in
3. Salt, whole white pepper, bay leaf, water
4. 500 g (17.5 oz) cabbage per kg (2 lb 3oz) meat

Instructions:

1. I brown the pieces of meat in butter in a large pot. The rest of the meat I fry in several rounds in a frying pan, and then put it in the pot.
2. When all the meat is in the pot, I deglaze the frying pan with water and add this to the pot. Then I add 10–20 white pepper corns and at least half a tablespoon salt. In addition I add 1–2 bay leaves and perhaps a bouillon cube.
3. Cover and turn down to low heat. Simmer.
4. An hour before it is time to eat, I add coarsely chopped cabbage and more water to the pot. When the cabbage is tender, the dish is ready. Chopped parsley sprinkled on top is good.

If you use twice as much meat as cabbage, the recipe has a fat burning quotient of 1.1. A large serving provides 500 kcal and about 3.5 g carbohydrates.

Swiss schnitzel with side dishes

In the 8+ group of recipes, there is a Swiss schnitzel that works just as well in the other groups. See the recipe on page 110. It contains only 1 g carbohydrates, so you can enjoy some side dishes. Unfortunately no green peas are allowed. They contain too many carbohydrates.

I can recommend brined anchovy butter, green salad, and a solid serving of tinned asparagus. You stay well within the limit of 6 g carbohydrates. Fat burning quotient: 0.7.

Vegetables au gratin with feta cheese cream

My wife prepares this dish. If you use feta cheese cream, it works well in the 4+ group.

Ingredients:

1. Mixed vegetables that grow above ground, for example courgette, aubergine, bell peppers, red chilli, onions, and fennel.
2. Olive oil
3. 150 g (5.5 oz) feta cheese
4. 100 g (3.5 oz) crème fraîche
5. 2 tbs basil
6. 1 finely chopped garlic clove
7. 2 tbs chopped parsley
8. Salt and pepper

Instructions:

1. Coarsely chop vegetables, mix, and put into a baking tray.
2. Drizzle with olive oil and sprinkle with salt and pepper.
3. Prepare a feta cheese cream of the remaining ingredients. Eat cold with the oven-baked vegetables, or add 100 ml (3.5 fl oz) cream and pour it over the vegetable before baking.
4. Bake the vegetables at 220 °C for less than 30 minutes.

A small portion of this dish contains about 150 calories and 3 g carbohydrates. Fat burning quotient: 2.0.

Coleslaw – the ultimate side dish in GI-Zero!

Coleslaw is an American cabbage salad, with onion, mayonnaise, lemon juice, and Dijon mustard. I often make large amounts, because everyone in the family likes it. It is perfect with fried meat or carbohydrate-free German sausage. And it suits fish as well as meat patties!

The salad isn't carbohydrate-free, but it is worth the eventual price you must pay. In the 4+ group, you can eat 100 g (3.5 oz), with 3.8 g carbohydrates. In the 2+ group, you can eat 150 g (5.5 oz), with 5.6 g carbohydrates. If you eat the salad with meat, you can eat 200 g (7 oz).

It just takes a few minutes to make this salad. I always have cabbage in the house. In a large bowl I mix:

1. 1 tbs Dijon mustard
2. 1 dash lemon juice
3. 100 ml (3.5 fl oz) crème fraîche
4. 100 ml (3.5 fl oz) mayonnaise
5. A good amount of black pepper

I use approximate amounts, which works fine. Then I finely chop a medium sized onion (yellow or red) and shred as much cabbage as the dressing will allow. The mixture mustn't be too dry; it should be sticky. Then I add more lemon juice or salt if necessary. The salad can be eaten at once, but it actually improves after a day or two in the refrigerator.

Salisbury steak with onions

Salisbury steak is delicious. I present a traditional recipe on page 94. It is based on the use of onion as a flavouring since the 8+ group must leave the onions on the plate. In the 4+ group you can eat a moderate amount of onions. If you put half a portion of fried onions (about 20 g) on each steak, you can eat three without exceeding your limit of 6 g carbohydrates.

Alternatively, you can drop the onion and add a side dish, for example the Florida salad on page 126. Then you have a completely different meal.

Cobbler's box is perfect for GI-Zero!

Skomakerlåda is a classic Swedish dish. In my youth, it was served everywhere, especially for lunch. Today the dish is almost forgotten. Combining salt pork, beef, and old-fashioned mashed potatoes with butter and cream is considered too unhealthy today. Interestingly enough, the generation that ate *skomakerlåda* were considerably less overweight than those who eat modern reduced-fat foods.

I can't eat potatoes because starch makes me fat. But I couldn't imagine staying away from *skomakerlåda*. So here is my GI-Zero! alternative.

Ingredients:
1. One good-sized steak per person
2. Lightly salted pork
3. Herb butter; for example, my anchovy butter
4. Mashed vegetables
5. Gherkins

Instructions:
1. Prepare mashed vegetables and herb butter.
2. Fry salt pork (you can also use bacon if you don't like fat). Keep warm.
3. Fry the steaks in the pork grease. Salt and pepper. I use a hot frying pan and fry them quickly.
4. You can serve the dish exactly as you please. I put the steak on a warm plate, add a serving of mashed vegetables, and top with the fried pork and herb butter. I also put some gherkins on the edge of the plate.

A *skomakerlåda* can contain anywhere from 500 to 1000 kcal. It depends on what kind of salt pork you use and how large a serving you eat. If you eat a 150 g (5.5 oz) steak, a half serving of salt pork, a normal serving of mashed vegetables, and 25 g (approx. 1 oz) herb butter, you have 750 kcal and 5.7 g carbohydrates. Fat burning quotient: 0.9.

Nettles are nice vegetables

I gather nettles with plastic gloves and soak them in water. Then I bring them to a quick boil together with a bouillon cube. I drain off the stock and drink as bouillon. Nettles actually contain as many healthy nutrients as vegetables once did a hundred years ago!

I put half of the blanched nettles in the freezer, and the other half serve as vegetables. Two pounds of fresh nettles yield 150 g blanched nettles. That is a good serving size.

Nettle soup

I sauté some mild onion and garlic in olive oil. Fifty grams (2 oz) of onions will do nicely. Then I add blanched nettles and continue to sauté the mixture. I add concentrated stock, let it all simmer, and round off with a solid dash of cream (when I talk about cream, I mean real, full-fat cream!).

I season with salt and pepper. A little grated lemon peel will provide extra zing. Sometimes I add a cheeseball or two. I make cheeseballs by mixing grated cheese with crème fraîche and a dash of cayenne pepper. Or I serve Airam's baked cheese crisps or some cheese macaroons.

Nettle soup alone contains 3–4 g carbohydrates per portion and a fat burning quotient of 3. The cream is the important ingredient! With a few cheese macaroons comes an additional gram of carbohydrates and protein. This pleasant meal provides about 400 calories per serving. Fat burning quotient: 2.

Creamed nettles

Creamed nettles are just as useful as spinach. Sauté the blanched nettles in butter, season, and add cream. Reduce to your desired consistency. A normal portion of creamed nettles contains only 2 g carbohydrates. Fat burning quotient: 5!

Meat soup with a side dish

Boil meat with vegetables according to taste. See page 111. As far as the 8+ group goes, I am adamant: eat the meat and leave the vegetables on your plate! The only vegetables allowed in this group are asparagus or cabbage.

The 4+ group, however, has more flexibility and should eat meat soup now and then. Especially if it includes bone marrow! What can you eat in addition? You can eat a small portion, 60–70 g (2–3 oz) of carrots. That adds 6 g carbohydrates. No other root vegetables are permitted, but you might also try:

1. 120 g (4 oz) cooked shallots or
2. 160 g (5.5 oz) cooked cabbage or
3. 175 g (6 oz) cooked cauliflower or
4. 200 g (7 oz) cooked broccoli or
5. 260 g (99 oz) cooked asparagus or
6. 600 g (21 oz) tinned asparagus

With one of these vegetables and two bowls of soup you have 600 kcal. Fat burning quotient: 0.7.

Quick soup accompaniments

Airam writes one of my favourite internet blogs. She presents many great recipes. Her baked cheese crisps are wonderful with soup or as a little cake with your coffee. Grab a cheese crisp when your friends offer you a cookie.

Baked cheese crisps

Instructions:

Turn the oven on to 250 °C. Beat together 2 eggs, 2 tbs mayonnaise, and 200 g (7 oz) grated cheese. Drop 8 table-spoons on a baking paper, not too close to each other, and put in the oven. After 7 minutes you have wonderful, golden brown, light cheese crisps. They can replace cakes, sweet rolls, and almost anything. And they are a fantastic accompaniment for soups.

One cheese crisp contains 100 kcal and 0.5 g carbohydrates. Fat burning quotient: 1.45.

Cheese macaroons

I came across this recipe in a newspaper. These are the simplest accompaniment to soup around. If your oven is already warm, you can make them when the soup is on the table.

Grate parmesan cheese and place in small piles on baking paper, about a tablespoon in each pile. Bake at 175 °C until they have a nice colour. That should take about 5 minutes. Be careful – these macaroons are quick to burn!

Cheese macaroons are perfect with mild soups, for example nettle soup. You can use any strong-tasting, hard type of cheese and probably some blue cheeses as well. Feta and haloumi don't work, as they won't spread out.

Salmon pâté with spinach

I present an excellent, low carbohydrate salmon pâté on page 104. It is primarily for the 8+ group. In the 4+ group, you get an additional 3 g carbohydrates to use. What should we do with them?

I suggest that you start by sautéing a package of spinach in butter. Add salt and pepper. Put the spinach in the bottom of a tray and fill with the pâté recipe on page 104. This is a complete and highly satisfying meal.

With 200 g (7 oz) sautéed spinach, 200 g (7 oz) salmon, and 2 tbs melted butter you have 900 kcal and 6 g carbohydrates. Fat burning quotient: 2.3.

My salsa

I like food that makes smoke puff out my ears, especially food seasoned with chilli peppers. I love to eat gherkins and jalapeños and always have a large jar of chilli paste in the refrigerator. If I don't have any of the above, I use a jar of piri-piri.

Piri-piri means "pepper-pepper" in Swahili. An appropriate name. But it isn't my favourite pepper because it has a sharp, thin taste. To achieve a full aroma that warms the front of your mouth and way down your throat, you need a combination of peppers.

Ingredients for the perfect salsa:
1. A package of mixed chillies – three or four kinds provides a fine, round flavour (alternatively, use some fresh chillies, some of my piri-piri, some tinned jalapeños, and a few tablespoons of chilli paste. But it isn't quite as good as the above).
2. Bell pepper, lemons, garlic, yellow onions, and chopped tomatoes.
3. Bouillon cubes.
4. Ground bell pepper, cumin, tarragon, and coriander are appropriate spices. But I can manage without them.

Instructions:

1. I finely chop the chillies and sauté them in coconut oil. If you prefer, you can also use olive oil or bacon grease. I want my salsa extra hot, so I use whole chillies including the seeds. People with sensitive taste buds should probably scrape away the insides of the chilli (add a few red and/or yellow bell peppers if you want the whole family to eat the salsa).

2. Turn down the heat, add some chopped garlic cloves and some chopped tomatoes. Then add a bouillon cube and a tablespoon of lemon juice. The secret of a good salsa is to balance the spicy and the sour. I use more lemon juice and less salt than most do, but it is a question of personal taste.

3. Now it is time to taste. If the chillies were of good quality, the salsa should burn like fire. Then I add the rest of the chopped tomatoes and perhaps some coarsely chopped bell pepper. It depends on the result that you want.

4. Now the salsa is under control. I add a few teaspoons of coriander and cumin, and sometimes a tablespoon of ground bell pepper. Sometimes I add oregano, sometimes not. Then I put the lid on the pan and let it stand.

Calculate that 100 ml (3.5 fl oz) salsa contains 3–4 g carbohydrates. But if you have made it really hot, 100 ml (3.5 fl oz) is quite a lot! Fat burning quotient: 0.9.

Meat patties with feta cheese and coleslaw

Meat patties with feta are one of our favourites. I offer an excellent recipe on page 92. The recipe is easy to make, and you don't need to weigh and measure. With sauce, it contains about 2 g carbohydrates per serving.

You have room for a side dish, and I suggest coleslaw (see page 133). 150 g (5.5 oz) of meat patties, some tablespoons of sauce, and a small portion of coleslaw provide 600 kcal and 5.7 g carbohydrates. The fat burning quotient is a fantastic 1.8!

Cheese-stuffed minced beef with tomato salad

I like to stuff minced meat with cheese. On page 94, I present a recipe for cheese-stuffed meat patties. A proper meat patty contains barely 1 g carbohydrates. Therefore, you could even include one of my side dishes in your meal.

I suggest a large meat patty (without cream sauce) and a small serving of tomato and onion salad. The meat patty can weigh 200 g (7 oz), and the salad should be less than 100 g (3.5 oz). That equals a small tomato, a quarter onion, and a dash of vinegar dressing.

This meal provides 650 kcal and 6 g carbohydrates, with a fat burning quotient of 6 g carbohydrates. If you replace the tomato salad with coleslaw, you save 1 g carbohydrates.

French green beans

I like French green beans. I use them in the following salad:

1. Quickly sauté beans in butter. Salt and pepper. Add one or two crushed garlic cloves.
2. Put into a bowl and cool.
3. Add finely chopped onion and dressing.

A small portion contains 100 calories and 3 g carbohydrates. Fat burning quotient: 2.6.

Broccoli and cheese au gratin

This vegetable casserole works for both 4+ and 2+. It can be eaten as an entrée or a side dish. I often eat it cold with cooked ham. In the 2+ group you can eat a large portion without exceeding the carbohydrate limit. And you will want to eat a large serving of this scrumptious dish!

Ingredients for filling:
1. 300 g (10.5 oz) broccoli
2. 100 g (3.5 oz) chopped flavourful cheese
3. 100 g (3.5 oz) chopped feta cheese

Ingredients for sauce:
1. 4 eggs
2. 200 ml (7 fl oz) full-fat milk
3. 200 ml (7 fl oz) cream
4. Seasoning, for example cayenne pepper. Salt and pepper if you want.

Instructions:
1. Blanch or defrost the broccoli. Drain.
2. Put into an oven-proof baking tray.
3. Distribute cheese over broccoli.
4. Mix sauce and pour over broccoli and cheese.
5. Bake at 200 °C until stiff and golden brown. This should take about 25 minutes.

A small 100 g (3.5 oz) serving contains 200 kcal and 2.7 g carbohydrates. Fat burning quotient: 1.4.

Pike and salmon pâté
Ingredients:
1. 600 g (1 lb 5 oz) fish fillets, for example half pike and half salmon
2. 6 eggs
3. 600 ml (just over 1 pint) cream
4. Seasoning; for example salt, white pepper, a dash of cayenne pepper, a dash of curry.

Instructions:

1. Run the fish through a blender or food processor.
2. Add seasonings, eggs, and cream.
3. Pour into greased oven-proof baking tray and cover with foil.
4. Bake in a casserole dish at 175 °C for about an hour.
5. Turn over on a serving dish and garnish with shrimp.

This dish is rich. A serving of 200 g (7 oz) provides 500 kcal and 3 g carbohydrates. Fat burning quotient: 1.6.

Serve with a classic shrimp sauce, or with a quick sauce of shrimp, crème fraîche, cream, caviar, and lemon juice. My shrimp sauce has about 1 g carbohydrates per dl (⅒ l) sauce. The quick sauce has twice the amount. The 8+ group can serve melted butter with the pâté.

A summary
of the 2+ program

Plate model for 2+:

Half the plate must be meat and half the plate can be greens. Vegetables that grow above ground can be eaten freely. An occasional root vegetable is allowed, preferably raw.

Carbohydrate limit: 9 g carbohydrates per meal, 27 g carbohydrates per day.

This is the most "liberal" form of GI-Zero! We could call it GI-Zero! with extras.

If you have followed the programs for 8+ and 4+ and arrived here, then you have every reason to be proud of your accomplishment. Congratulations! Unfortunately, you are probably still insulin resistant. This means that you release too much insulin when your blood sugar levels rise. You can use the 2+ program, but you can't eat more liberally than 2+.

However, if you have started with the 2+ program, being 2 stone (13 kg) or less overweight, you probably still have normal sensitivity to insulin. Your pancreas releases a normal amount of insulin when your blood sugar levels rise, and you don't have to be so restrictive. However, the more liberal your diet, the more you have to control your intake of calories. If you start to eat whole wheat bread, which I don't recommend, you are practicing a traditional GI diet. Then you have to watch both your calories and your fat intake!

Another important difference, compared the other GI-

Zero! groups, is that you can eat as much protein as you want. You don't need to supplement lean meat with fat if you don't want to. In terms of energy percentages, you can consume 35 percent protein, 55–60 percent fat, and 5–10 percent carbohydrates.

As a general rule:

You can eat everything from the 8+ group and add lots of side dishes. You can eat everything from the 4+ group and often double the side dish allowance for that group. If you are only just overweight, or not at all, I recommend that you get regular exercise, preferably in fresh air. Fresh air and sunshine are very important for health and well-being.

A normal day on 2+

You can eat about 30 g carbohydrates per day. I eat this much forone or two days every month at the most. Modest servings of my common side dishes contain 2–5 g carbohydrates. Even if I eat something green with every meal, I try not to exceed 20 g carbohydrates per day. At the moment, I eat carbohydrate-free meals during the day and lots of greens for dinner.

I always try to keep my intake of carbohydrates low because I primarily eat animal products. To my way of thinking, vegetables that grow above ground are flavourful side dishes, but never a main part of a meal. You can fill half your plate with meat and the other half with greens if you want, but select the greens sensibly.

On page 70, I present an informative list. You can see that 60–65 g (2.5 oz) parsnips or carrots contain as many carbohydrates as 200 g (7 oz) cooked broccoli or 600 g (21 oz) tinned asparagus. Not to mention spinach! You can eat quite a bit of sautéed spinach in exchange for a small carrot.

Your most common side dishes should still be based on vegetables that grow above ground. If you really want something crispy, you should choose common radishes instead of carrots and beetroot. A small cooked carrot contains as many carbohydrates as 75 normal-sized radishes!

My measurements provide you with a high degree of freedom. Of course you shouldn't eat bread, pasta, and potatoes, not even in small portions, because starch is harmful. It is possible that you can tackle these large glucose molecules without gaining weight, but they still won't offer you the best possible health.

You can use all the recipes in the 2+ group, and of course the more low carbohydrate recipes for the 4+ and 8+ groups. In addition, all my general recipes are permitted. You can use many recipes from normal cookbooks. The difference is that you replace root vegetables and grain products with vegetables that grow above ground. Instead of potatoes, you eat butter-cooked broccoli or ratatouille. And you must not thicken your sauces with flour; use egg yolks instead. Then you can just enjoy your meal.

An example of a simple menu follows:

Breakfast

Quick shrimp and avocado salad, tuna fish salad, or bacon omelette; see the section on breakfasts from page 33. Or why not try a quick salad of roast beef and greens? You can find a suggestion on page 169. If you ate cheese soufflé yesterday, a reheated serving is an interesting alternative. That is a favourite of mine in the morning. The recipe is on page 150.

Lunch (when you are hungry, not because it is noon)

You are probably aware that you can fry cold-smoked salmon in a frying pan. It is an excellent 5 minute meal. Sauté the salmon with spinach or something similar, and add 100 g

(3.5 oz) crème fraîche. Reduce. Add freshly ground pepper and the dish is ready to serve.

A good portion provides 600 kcal and 5 g carbohydrates. Fat burning quotient: 1.7. That is primarily the spinach; if you select another vegetable, you will have a few additional carbohydrates.

If you eat lunch out, the same rules apply. You can eat as much as you want of the meat you have ordered, and in addition you can select vegetables that have grown above ground from the salad bar. Bread, pasta, and potatoes don't belong in your meals at all.

Dinner

For dinner you have a lot of freedom. I would probably choose a real piece of meat with herb butter and ratatouille. You can eat as much as you want of this food. Or why not a liver dish? We should eat liver every week! Chicken liver contains the smallest amount of carbohydrates. I present an excellent recipe in this book. If you have been careful with your carbohydrate consumption during the course of the day, you can even eat fried liver. A solid serving of this dish provides 16 g carbohydrates, but it is worth it!

You could, of course, point out that 16 g carbohydrates are not allowed in a single meal. In normal situations this is true, but there is nothing to stop you from saving your carbohydrates until dinner. Some dishes are so healthy that their nutritional value outweighs any issues with their carbohydrate content. After all, GI-Zero! is primarily a program for good health.

Those who dislike liver often like fish. Why this is so I don't know. I present some simple recipes for baked fish on page 153. You will like them!

Recipes for 2+

Clear the way for side dishes!

In the 2+ group 9 g carbohydrates are allowed per meal. We don't *require* 9 g per meal, we *allow* 9 g. The fewer carbohydrates the better!

If you have worked your way into this group from the 8+ group, you will notice that there is more freedom and flexibility in the 2+ group. For those of you who start in this group, the program can seem restrictive. However you will adjust to it as your taste preferences change!

I find 9 g carbohydrates per meal is quite a lot. I didn't eat more than that in an entire day for most of my weight loss period. I lost 7 stone (45 kg) in 9 months. Even today, if I eat 9 g carbohydrates per meal I am at the limit of what I can tolerate and still keep my present weight.

If you are starting your weight loss journey in the 2+ group, and are not as carbohydrate-sensitive as I am, you can eat these 9 g carbohydrates without a problem – perhaps even more than that. But begin by maintaining this limit until you have achieved your weight loss goal. Then you can experiment to find out how many carbohydrates you can tolerate.

Generally speaking, this is my advice to all groups in the GI-Zero! program. Complete your weight loss first and experiment afterwards. If you start testing alternatives before your body has managed to adapt to a new regime of fat metabolism, you are asking for trouble.

How much is 9 g carbohydrates per meal? It corresponds to 3 avocado halves or a large serving of spinach with cream cheese or cream. Or a large plateful of Greek salad. However, such vegetable orgies mean that the rest of your food must be free from carbohydrates, and that is seldom the case. If you eat 200 g (7 oz) of shrimp, a tablespoon of mayonnaise, an egg, and a slice of lemon, you have consumed 2.6 g carbohydrates. Perhaps you were not aware of this, but carbohydrates are present in most foods. Even so, that meal is relatively low in carbohydrates, and you can fill the rest of your plate with a mixed green salad and dressing without exceeding the 9 g carbohydrates.

In practice, this means that you can use all the recipes in the 8+ group and choose a good amount of green in addition. If you start with a recipe from the 4+ group, you can't add as much green.

Here's an example. Look at the beef stroganoff recipe in the 4+ group (page 125). In that version, the dish contains 6 g carbohydrates per portion. That is quite a bit, but you can still supplement your serving with half an avocado (2.6 g carbohydrates) and some green leaves (or you can drop the side dish and use more onions and cream in the stroganoff).

If you choose the low carbohydrate version with a touch of beef stroganoff (page 105), you have room for half an avocado and a green salad. Alternatively, you could try a large portion of mashed broccoli (page 122) or a portion of coleslaw (page 133). I prefer to eat a more flavourful beef stroganoff, even though I can only supplement with green leaves.

My most important side dishes:
1. Creamed spinach, 2 g carbohydrates, page 99.
2. Florida salad, 2.5 g carbohydrates, page 126.
3. Half an avocado with a tsp lemon juice, 3 g carbohydrates.

4. My mashed vegetables, 3.25 g carbohydrates, page 123.
5. Frittata, 3.6 g carbohydrates for 3 pieces, page 74.
6. Coleslaw, 3.8 g carbohydrates, page 133.
7. Ratatouille, 3 g carbohydrates, page 129.
8. Tomato and onion salad, about 5 g carbohydrates, page 172.
9. Greek salad, 6 g carbohydrates, page 152.

The values for most of these are based on 100 g (3.5 oz) servings. That isn't very much. If you eat twice that amount, you have twice as many carbohydrates!

Cheese soufflé

Previously I mentioned cheese soufflé as a suggestion for breakfast. I admit to a childish enthusiasm for cheese soufflé! This recipe actually contains a little flour – very few of my recipes do, but this is one of them. Consider it an exception that proves the rule!

Many soufflés are tricky to prepare, but not this one. At any rate not when you follow the recipe. You can make soufflé from stiffly beaten egg whites and mayonnaise too, but that belongs in a course for the advanced. Here we choose the safe version. Make a large batch!

For 6 servings you need:
1. 3 tbs butter
2. 300 ml (10.5 fl oz) skimmed milk
3. 3 tbs potato starch
4. 6 eggs, separated
5. 200–250 g (7–8.5 oz) grated cheese, preferably quite flavourful
6. Nutmeg, cayenne pepper, salt

Instructions:

1. Melt the butter on low heat and mix in the milk and potato starch. Stir well and set the pan to the side when the mixture has thickened.
2. Mix in the egg yolks and cheese. Season according to taste.
3. Beat the egg whites. I do it by hand in a round bowl – but, of course, you can use a food processor. A pinch of salt hastens the process. Beat the egg whites so stiff that you can turn the bowl upside down and nothing runs out. Stiff egg whites are the secret to success!
4. Have you greased the soufflé tray? If not, do it now. And check to see that the oven is set to 175 °C.
5. Now carefully fold the stiff egg whites into the cooled cheese mixture. Use the spatula. Do not stir! Now, put the soufflé into the oven.
6. Set the timer for 35 minutes. When the time has passed you can take a quick look. The soufflé will probably need another 5 minutes. If you open the oven door too soon, you risk the masterpiece collapsing!

A standard serving provides 350 kcal and 8.4 g carbohydrates. With a tablespoon of melted butter it is 450 kcal and a fat burning quotient of 1.3. One more tablespoon of butter and the fat burning quotient is 1.7.

Strömmingsflundror (double fillets of herring stuffed with dill or parsley) with coleslaw

If you belong to the 2+ group you can enjoy this rustic Swedish food. Recipes abound in old cookbooks. We can eat as much meat and fish as we want, but we have to limit the side dishes. We should also avoid potatoes and sauces thickened with flour.

Breadcrumbed herring is delicious. It contains fewer

carbohydrates than you think, but for safety's sake the bread-crumbs should consist of rye flour. Ground, deep-fried bacon rinds are even better, but you might not always have them available. This is my second recipe that contains flour. There are no more than these two!

Instructions:
1. I put something good on a *herring* fillet, perhaps an anchovy and some chopped greens, like dill, parsley, or chives, whatever you wish. Salt and pepper. Then, press the second fillet together with the first.
2. I breadcrumb this double-decker with some seasoned rye flour, without using an egg. You can mix in a little ground rusk if you like.
3. Fry the fillets in a hot frying pan.

You will find the coleslaw recipe on page 133. Make the salad ahead of time, preferably the day before.

A portion of *strömmingsflundror* (100 g, 3.5 oz) and a small portion of coleslaw (100 g, 3.5 oz) provides 8 g carbo-hydrates. Fat burning quotient: 1.3.

Greek salad

A Greek salad is a good side dish in the 2+ group. I often use this at dinner. A Greek salad normally consists of onion, tomato or bell pepper, cucumber, feta cheese, and olives. Olive oil and lemon juice constitute the dressing. Coarsely ground pepper is an absolute must – but, other than that, you can vary the salad endlessly. Some have said that there is a Greek salad for every Greek island. I use bell peppers to save carbohydrates (bell peppers contain as many carbo-hydrates as tomatoes do per weight, but you can get by with less bell pepper). Some bell pepper rings in different colours and some cucumber pieces are a good beginning. On top of that I sprinkle finely chopped onion, olives, and some chunks of feta cheese. Then I squeeze a lemon over the salad, sprinkle with olive oil, and finish with a few turns of the pepper grinder.

If you dislike raw onions, you can marinate the onions in oil, lemon juice, and seasoning for a while, and then mix the salad in the marinade.

A normal serving usually contains about 6 g carbohydrates. The fat burning quotient ends up at 2.5. Add half an avocado, and you have an additional 2.6 g carbohydrates. A salad like this is permissible in the 2+ group. Eating it together with a lamb chop is also allowed!

Baked fish

Baked fish is simple food. Simple to make anyway. The taste can be as complex as you like.

Instructions:
1. Put the fish in a baking tray.
2. Salt and pepper. Squeeze lemon juice over the fish.
3. Pour on a sauce of cream, and bake the fish at 225 °C. Could it be any easier?

You decide what you want to mix in the cream, but the cream should dominate. I usually use a free combination of crème fraîche, mayonnaise, cheese, and egg yolks. I flavour with Dijon mustard.

This is an approved food for all groups. In the 8+ group you eat primarily the fish and sauce. In the other groups there is room for side dishes.

Zander au gratin with tarragon flavour

Would you like the world's easiest recipe for zander fillets? Here it is!

1. Put some zander fillets close together in a greased oven-proof tray. Salt and pepper and squeeze lemon juice over the fish.
2. Mix cream, some grated cheese, and an egg yolk, and pour over the fish.
3. Finally, sprinkle with lots of fresh tarragon.
4. Bake at 225 °C until the fish is golden brown. This should take about 20 minutes.
5. Choose an appropriate side dish, perhaps Mervis' creamed spinach (page 99). Asparagus always tastes good, and you can eat as much of it as you like!

A solid 200 g (7 oz) serving plus sauce provides 600 kcal and 3 g carbohydrates. Fat burning quotient: 1.1.

Baked mayonnaise salmon

I found this recipe on the internet. We had it for a dinner with some students recently, and it was popular with all age groups.

1. Rub half a salmon with salt and chopped dill.
2. Spread with mayonnaise.
3. Bake in oven for 30 minutes.

Calculate 600–800 kcal for a good size serving. The dish contains less than 0.5 g carbohydrates and has a fat burning quotient of 2. Spinach is a good side dish.

Airam's Boursin chicken with vegetables

With 9 g carbohydrates per meal you have relatively free hands. You can make meat dishes that contain some carbohydrates – for example, beef stroganoff – and then reduce your amount of greens. But you can also choose a low carbohydrate entrée and supplement with lots of greens.

Airam's Boursin chicken is a good starting point. See the recipe on page 112.

This is a flavourful recipe that suits a large green salad. It is also great with coleslaw.

A serving of chicken with sauce contains 600 kcal and less than 2 g carbohydrates. You can add fried vegetables or a Greek salad without exceeding 9 g carbohydrates.

Ham casserole with side dish

If you have progressed through the 8+ and 4+ groups, you have grown accustomed to preparing casseroles, the easiest meals of all! For those of you who are starting in the 2+ group, I will provide a brief introduction.

Making casseroles from different fish and meat leftovers is a classic method. These were the dishes that tasted so good when you used to visit your grandmother. You can use all kinds of meat, fish, and poultry as a basis. Salmon, herring, lamb, chicken, ham, or minced meat – all work just as well.

The principle is simple. You mix one part meat and one part cheese and cream. Then you bake in the oven at around 225 °C until golden brown. On page 108 I present a recipe for a ham casserole. It contains 2.6 g carbohydrates. You can add 5–6 g carbohydrates to the meal, but you don't have to!

150 g (5.5 oz) of a vegetable of your choice – one that grows above ground – cooked in butter and mixed with cream provides 6 g carbohydrates and a fat burning quotient of 1.5. Or you can choose 300 g (10.5 oz) of Mervis' creamed spinach. Then you add 5.4 g carbohydrates and come up to 8 g altogether. Fat burning quotient: 1.36.

Pepper stuffed with minced meat

Green bell peppers are an approved food. There are 3 g carbohydrates in a large bell pepper, and fewer if you remove the flesh and seeds. We can stuff the bell pepper with a good minced meat and have a complete meal that contains less than 9 g per serving.

Ingredients:
1. Large green bell pepper
2. My Wallenberg mixture or other minced meat
3. Sugar-free tomato purée
4. Stock
5. Butter

Instructions:

Purchase some really large green bell peppers and as much pork mince as you need.

Cut off the bottom of the peppers and around the stem. Keep these lids. Remove the flesh and seeds, and rinse.

Make a ground meat mixture. Season the ground meat to taste. In the past, I have used chopped jalapeños, and I like that. Perhaps you would prefer crumbled feta cheese or onions?

Stuff the bell peppers with the minced meat mixture and put the lids on again. Fasten with toothpicks if necessary.

Melt butter in a pan, preferably a tall pan with a lid. Add stock and mix in a few tablespoons of sugar-free tomato purée. I found this idea in an old cookbook and it works really well.

Place the stuffed pepper in the pan, cover, and let simmer at medium heat for 30–40 minutes. When the pepper is tender, your meal is ready.

One large stuffed pepper with sauce contains about 500 kcal and 7 g carbohydrates. Fat burning quotient: 2.4. Garnish med lettuce. Red endive salad is good.

Luxurious oven baked Wallenbergs in an oven pan

Dining on Wallenbergs offers a glimpse of the good life, but preparing them according to the recipe involves a sticky mess. The original recipe calls for an egg yolk and 100 ml (3.5 fl oz) cream for each 100 g (3.5 oz) minced veal. If you have tried this, you know well the sticky mess to which I refer.

When I make real Wallenbergs, I reduce the amount of cream and egg yolks. Four hundred grams (14 oz) minced veal to 3 egg yolks and 300 ml (10.5 fl oz) cream produces a mixture that is far easier to handle. This is how the Swedish cook Cattelin prepared his version. Food writer and cookbook author Pernilla Tunberger keeps the egg yolks, but removes another 100 ml (3.5 fl oz) of cream.

If you really want to follow the original recipe, here is a good solution – run the mixture through a food processor and bake in the oven!

Ingredients:
1. 1 kg (2 lb, 3 oz) finely minced veal
2. 10 egg yolks
3. 1 litre (approx 2 pints) cream
4. Salt and pepper
5. Butter for frying

Shape into a loaf in the oven pan and bake at 225 °C for about 50 minutes. Remember that Wallenbergs aren't supposed to be hard and dry!

Remove the loaf, pour the drippings into a pan, and reduce. When properly thick, add cream to get the desired consistency.

This is an elegant and calorie-rich dish. If you cut the loaf into ten slices, each will provide 700 kcal and 4.6 g carbohydrates. Fat burning quotient: 2.5.

Select your side dish. I suggest creamed spinach or mashed broccoli. If you take an average serving, you have room for some spears of asparagus as well.

Steak with mustard sauce

I often eat steak with mustard sauce, pepper sauce, or cheese sauce. The principle is always the same. I fry the meat and use the pan drippings as the basis for a sauce. While I stir, I deglaze the pan with a liquid, usually stock or wine, add cream and seasoning, and reduce.

For example:
1. Fry a steak in butter. Put it on a warm plate or in the oven.
2. Sauté the accompaniment – small onions and mush-rooms, chillies, and bell pepper, or whatever you want.
3. Add some wine or stock to the pan. Stir. Add cream and season with Dijon mustard and garlic. I use half a table-spoon mustard; you might prefer to use a teaspoon.
4. Reduce and pour over the steak.

This dish becomes what you make of it. With a 150 g (5.5 oz) beef and a good amount of side dish you have 700 kcal and 7–9 g carbohydrates. Fat burning quotient: 1.0.

Vegetables au gratin

You can prepare all kinds of vegetables au gratin with the help of cheese, cream, and butter.

1. Put a good amount of vegetables in a greased oven-proof baking tray.
2. Pour over a warm mixture of cream, cheese, and butter.
3. Put some cheese slices on top.
4. Bake at 200 °C until golden brown.

A small portion provides 350 kcal and 4–5 g carbohydrates. Fat burning quotient: 2. I use a lot of cream and probably reach a fat burning quotient of 3.

Salad niçoise

Tuna fish salad is a common dish in Mediterranean countries.

Ingredients:
1. Tinned tuna fish
2. Hardboiled egg
3. Brined anchovies
4. Black olives
5. French dressing
6. Some onion
7. Some lettuce
8. Fresh dill

Instructions:
1. I put the dressing in the bottom of the bowl and add the chopped onions. They marinate in the dressing before it is time to eat.
2. Then I add the tuna fish, about half a tin per person, right in the centre of the bowl. If there are a lot of you, there will be a small mountain of tuna fish!
3. I place the lettuce around the tuna fish and garnish with egg slices, olives, and brined anchovies. I then sprinkle with fresh dill.

This salad keeps well in the refrigerator (mixed salads wilt faster).

A normal serving of our salad niçoise contains 600 kcal and 6–7 g carbohydrates. Fat burning quotient: 1.4. If you use tuna fish in water, the fat burning quotient will be lower.

Pork shank with mashed root vegetables

Here we have a classic meal that is within the limits of 9 g carbohydrates. The prerequisites are that you eat a small serving of the mashed root vegetables and that you don't use potatoes. Potatoes contain 18 g carbohydrates per 100 g. Swedes have a third of that amount!

Ingredients:
1. Lightly salted pork shank
2. Yellow onions
3. Seasoning to taste. Classic recipes contain good amounts of pepper, cloves, and bay leaf. I am a little careful with these "Christmas spices" and use pepper and thyme instead. Salt is unnecessary.
4. Swede
5. A small carrot
6. Butter

Instructions:
1. Blanch the pork shank and change the water.
2. Let the shank simmer with the onion and seasoning until the meat separates from the bone. This takes 2 hours.
3. Boil swede cut into large pieces together with the carrot in some of the stock. When the vegetables are tender, drain and mix with butter.
4. Eat the pork shank and a reasonable serving of mashed swede with Dijon mustard.

One portion of 150 g (5.5 oz) pork shank, 100 g (3.5 oz) mashed vegetables, and a tablespoon Dijon mustard provides 600 kcal and 7 g carbohydrates. Fat burning quotient: 0.9.

Baked omelette
with fried smoked ham and mushrooms

I am an eager mushroom picker. When I come home with a good basket of chanterelles, I often make a mushroom omelette. If it is just for myself, I use the frying pan, but let's say I have some summer guests. It has to be an oven omelette!

Instructions:
1. Turn oven on to 225 °C.
2. If the chanterelles are fresh, start with them. They have to be dehydrated at low heat before you can sauté them.
3. Beat together 6 eggs and 400 ml (14 fl oz) cream, or there about. Add salt and pepper. Pour into a greased oven-proof tray. Bake for 15 minutes, at the most 17–18 minutes.
4. While the omelette bakes, sauté the mushrooms and fry the ham. Talk about a perfect summer meal!

A good serving contains 600 kcal and 5 g carbohydrates. Fat burning quotient: 1.2.

Fried mixed mushrooms

Mushrooms are excellent side dishes for meat and fish. 100 g (3.5 oz) fresh mushrooms contain about 4 g carbohydrates, some vitamins, iron, potassium, and phosphorus.

Raw mushrooms have a low fat burning quotient. If you eat mushrooms raw, you should sprinkle them with olive oil. Sautéed mushrooms soak up fat and have a fat burning quotient of about 2.

I like to pick mushrooms, and I make all sorts of mushroom dishes. I eat modest portions, but even a small serving of mushrooms provides a lot of flavour.

The wonderful thing about mushrooms is that you can mix more or less all kinds of mushrooms together and the taste just gets better and better. Strangely enough, though, there are many people who find it difficult to sauté mushrooms. The basic mistake that people make is to start with too low temperature and too moist mushrooms. Or perhaps they have too many mushrooms in the pan at a time. That way, it is difficult to achieve a good result.

The best way is first to dehydrate the mushrooms on low heat in a large pan. Let some time pass, minimum 10–15 minutes. Then melt the fat in a frying pan and add appropriate amounts of mushrooms. When the mushrooms have good colour, turn down the heat, and season to taste. Salt, pepper, and a crushed garlic clove work well. Perhaps some chervil or chives. If you want to cream the mushrooms, add cream or crème fraîche and reduce. Sprinkle with chopped parsley and serve.

Calculate that a serving of sautéed mushrooms (75 g, 2.5 oz) provides 4 g carbohydrates. Fat burning quotient: 2. With a bit of cream you can add an additional carbohydrate, and the fat burning quotient comes up to 3.

Cheese-stuffed minute steak with mushrooms

I present a great recipe for cheese-stuffed minute steak on page 103. Why not continue to sauté mushrooms – and perhaps some onions – in the same pan? Then add cream and pour the sauce over the meat.

Cheese-stuffed minute steak with this mushroom sauce contains 500 kcal and 8 g carbohydrates. Fat burning quotient: 1.0.

My mushroom omelette

My mushroom omelette is very popular with my friends. I often make it when we come home from mushroom picking. The recipe has an Italian character. The idea is to use the herbs in your kitchen garden, preferably 6 to 8 different herbs, with parsley as the basis.

I do the same with my mushroom omelette. Consider the recipe below as a suggestion only. You can vary all the ingredients, with the exception of the mushrooms and the eggs.

Ingredients:
1. Fresh mushrooms
2. 6 eggs
3. Lots of fresh herbs. Often a handful of parsley, a bundle of chives plus French tarragon, basil, and lemon thyme. Perhaps a handful of spinach too.
4. Bacon. The original recipe is an omelette with mushrooms, but we need a little more from the animal world!

Instructions:
1. Dehydrate the mushrooms in a pot. Fry the bacon.
2. Put the bacon aside and sauté the mushrooms in the same pan. Add a chopped onion if you want.
3. When the mushrooms are half done, add the herbs. It will be a large pile, but they sink down. I usually add a little oil from a jar of sun-dried tomatoes. Or my own mushroom oil if I have some.
4. When the greens have sunken down and you start to see the mushrooms again, add the beaten eggs and a dash of cream. I stir around with the spatula to avoid making a pancake. The temperature shouldn't be too high.
5. Finally I sprinkle with the bacon and some chopped olives.

A good portion of this omelette, including the bacon, provides 600 kcal and 9 g carbohydrates. Fat burning quotient: 1.2.

Quick mushroom salad

1. Fry chopped bacon.
2. Distribute some green leaves on a few plates.
3. When the bacon is done, add finely sliced mushrooms of the kind that you can eat raw. Champignons, porcinos, or large parasol mushrooms work well. Turn the mushrooms carefully. They shouldn't be sautéed, just warmed in the bacon grease, and they should look fresh!
4. Sprinkle French dressing on the lettuce and distribute the mushrooms and bacon.

This is a delicious appetiser. An average serving provides 300 kcal, 3 g carbohydrates, and a fat burning quotient of 2.5.

Antipasti is GI-Zero!

The Italians keep their shape. This must be due to their antipasti! If you wonder what antipasti means, it is what comes before the pasta. Or more correctly, before the meal. We would call it an appetiser.

Antipasti often contains mushrooms in some form or another, for example brined porcinos. Plus many other titbits that work well in the GI-Zero! program. Prosciutto di Parma, Bresaola ham, salami, and green olives. I consider this recipe a complete lunch!

Ingredients:

1. Small, crisp porcinos
2. Vinegar, lemon juice
3. Seasoning to taste, for example garlic, bay leaf, and thyme.

Instructions:

1. Slice the mushrooms lengthwise to keep their shape. You should be able to see that they are porcinos!

2. Blanch the sliced mushrooms in a marinade of vinegar, lemon juice, and seasonings according to taste. I use salt, white pepper, and bay leaf. Perhaps a crushed garlic clove. Perhaps some thyme.
3. When the mushrooms have cooled, mix them with a good olive oil in a clean jar. I am careful with hygiene to achieve a good result.
4. Then I let the mushrooms stand in a cool place for a month or two. It will keep as long as the jar is unopened, but when you have opened the jar you have a week to use it up. Keep the oil! It is excellent in salad dressings and omelettes.

When you've practiced the recipe a number of times and become really good at it, I suggest that you visit a store that carries Italian delicacies, and buy some Prosciutto di Parma, Bresaola ham, and some thick slices of Italian salami. And some good cheese. Put these on a large serving plate and set out some jars of olives and mushrooms. Then give me a call!

The nutritional content of this meal depends on what you eat. It will be difficult to get up to 9 g carbohydrates. The food is salty, and your body will retain water. Don't pay any attention to the bathroom scales the next day. You might gain weight on antipasti, but you aren't gaining fat.

Grilled salmon with side dish

Grilled salmon is a tasty, simple, and inexpensive food. Salmon is a fatty fish with a good fat burning quotient. And it contains no carbohydrates. Therefore, you have a lot of freedom to choose side dishes. I prefer to eat a large serving of creamed vegetables with this grilled fish.

Instructions:
1. Make a good herb butter and put it in the refrigerator.
2. Start up the grill.

3. Prepare the vegetable side dish, for example creamed spinach. I would also enjoy two avocado halves with lemon juice. It's up to you.
4. Season the salmon. I use salt and pepper.
5. Grill the salmon on both sides until it has nice colour. This usually takes 3–4 minutes per side. Make a small incision to check if the fish is done.
6. Put the salmon and creamed vegetables on a serving dish and put a slice of herb butter on each piece. Garnish with lemon wedges.

A good serving provides 700 kcal and 5 g carbohydrates. Fat burning quotient: 1.2. (If you choose 2 half avocados instead of the creamed spinach, there will be 3 g carbohydrates. Fat burning quotient: 1.3).

Chicken salad with bacon

1. Brown and bake a chicken as you normally would (I season, brown it in a pot, and set the pot in the oven at 200 °C. It takes less than 30 minutes.)
2. While the chicken is in the oven, I fry the bacon until crispy and chop some vegetables: iceberg lettuce, cucumber, and green bell peppers are good. Perhaps some shallots.
3. I cut the chicken into large pieces and mix them with the vegetables. Then I sprinkle with French dressing and garnish with the bacon bits.
4. A good serving of this delicious salad contains 550 kcal and 5–6 g carbohydrates. Fat burning quotient 1.

If you have a Florida salad in the refrigerator, you can simply expand it with chicken. Then you have a low carbohydrate salad with only 2.2 g carbohydrates per serving. Fat burning quotient: 1.4.

A small anchovy dish

When it is hot in the summer you need something salty. Anchovies fit the bill. Together with chopped hardboiled egg, onion, and dressing, they are a pleasant summer dish.

Ingredients:
1. Anchovy fillets, about 5 per serving
2. Hardboiled eggs
3. Yellow onion
4. Parsley
5. French dressing

1. Distribute the anchovies in the centre of a plate.
2. Chop the other ingredients and place them in a ring around the fillets.
3. Sprinkle with French dressing and set in the refrigerator for 30 minutes.

A normal portion with one egg and five fillets contains less than 400 kcal and 9 g carbohydrates. Fat burning quotient: 1.5. If this is not enough for you, eat more eggs and fewer fillets. In principle you can eat as many eggs as you want to in the GI-Zero! program.

Chicken liver with mushrooms and salt pork

Liver is a fantastic GI-Zero! food. The advantage of chicken liver is that it contains so few carbohydrates. Therefore you have room for a diverse selection of delicious side dishes.

Ingredients:
1. 300 g (10.5 oz) chicken liver
2. Half a package lightly salted pork
3. Mushrooms to taste
4. A yellow or red onion

5. A garlic clove
6. Butter for frying
7. Lots of finely chopped parsley
8. Stock
9. My mashed broccoli, recipe on page 122.
10. Salt, pepper, and appropriate herbs, for example thyme and marjoram

Instructions:

I start with the mashed broccoli because it takes the most time.

While the broccoli cooks, I fry the salt pork and set it aside.

Then I continue with the mushrooms and the onion. I mix them with the salt pork.

Now the broccoli is ready. I mix it with butter and cream.

Then I brown the chicken liver on all sides, salt and season. When the liver is a good colour, add the salt pork, mushroom, and onion, and add some stock. After a few more minutes, the dish is ready to eat.

If you have the opportunity to enter this into some nutritional software, you will see how all the values point upward, with large amounts of vitamin A and folic acid and all the B vitamins. There are large amounts of vitamin C too. If you were to get the same amount of vitamin C from apples, you would also have consumed 100 g sugar!

A good portion of this excellent dish contains 700 kcal and 9 g carbohydrates. Fat burning quotient: 1.0.

Cheese-stuffed minute steak with side dish of choice

I want to beat the drum for my cheese-stuffed minute steak, recipe on page 103. They are perfect eaten warm or cold, and they can be combined with a wide range of side dishes. Perfect hiking food, perfect in your lunch box, and perfect when you need something quick to eat. With ready-to-eat cheese-stuffed minute steak in your freezer and refrigerator you can tackle any unexpected situation.

Best of all, they taste great. You must only remember to fry at least double the amount you need. Soon you will have a bank that you can make withdrawals from every time you need fast food!

A medium piece contains 240 kcal and only 0.9 g carbohydrates. Fat burning quotient: 0.6. You can eat two pieces of stuffed minute steak and still have room for some really scrumptious side dishes. You can choose almost anything from my list of side dishes.

I like to combine two pieces of stuffed minute steak with a medium sized serving of coleslaw and half an avocado, for 760 kcal and 9 g carbohydrates. Fat burning quotient: 0.85.

If you eat two pieces of stuffed minute steak and a Greek salad, you have 850 kcal, 8.6 g carbohydrates, and a fat burning quotient of 1.

Roast beef salad

In the 2+ group you can mix meat and vegetables that grow above ground in salads with few restrictions. You can eat as much meat as you want, and then select the vegetables on the basis of carbohydrate content. You can consider tinned asparagus as a "free" vegetable, and cucumbers and green leaves as almost free. For colour you can use bell pepper instead of tomatoes, since bell pepper rings weigh half as much as tomato wedges do. French dressing is an obvious choice. As a rule, make sure that a third of the salad is meat!

A few days ago, I opened the refrigerator and found some leftover roast beef and coleslaw. Normally I would eat these together, perhaps with some grated horseradish. But it was summer, and I made a salad. I made it just for myself; the amounts are therefore:

1. 200 g (7 oz) roast beef
2. A little coleslaw (100 g, 3.5 oz)
3. 1 tin asparagus
4. A handful iceberg lettuce
5. Some bell pepper rings
6. Some chunks of cucumber
7. Pepper and my French dressing. (A few tablespoons of classic French dressing contains 0.4 g carbohydrates, recipe on page 54. Shop-bought French dressing can contain 10 times as much!)

This meal has 600 kcal, less than 9 g carbohydrates, and a fat burning quotient of 0.75. The high proportion of protein reduces the fat burning quotient, but that isn't a problem in this group. Here, most people can tolerate the high proportion of protein without releasing extra insulin.

Lars Wilson's lamb liver

Biologist and nutritional writer Lars Wilson and I have become friends. He has written books about Stone Age* diets. Lars is a great cook, and his lamb liver is a real delicacy.

Ingredients:
1. Lamb liver
2. 1 package bacon
3. Onion
4. 300 ml (10.5 fl oz) cream
5. Season according to taste

Instructions:
- Chop the bacon and brown in a pot.
- Remove the bacon and continue to brown the chopped onions in the bacon grease.

* pre-historic

- Remove the onions and continue to brown the liver. Season.
- Put the bacon and onion back in the pot.
- Pour in 300 ml (10.5 fl oz) cream and reduce.

I usually add crushed juniper berries and rosemary when I make lamb or reindeer/moose casseroles. I don't think Lars Wilson has any problems with this.

One serving of this casserole contains between 500 and 600 kcal and 7 g carbohydrates. You have room for a serving of sautéed spinach.

English fried liver

English fried liver is one of my absolute favourite dishes. Healthier food is hard to find. There is, however, one problem with this dish. It contains far too many carbohydrates. English fried liver is made with calf liver or beef liver plus bacon, onions, capers, Dijon mustard, and vinegar. Everything except the bacon contains carbohydrates, and the liver contains the most. 150 g (5.5 oz) of fried beef liver contains 8 g carbohydrates! Along with normal side dishes, a standard serving will contain 16 g carbohydrates.

So what do you do? You could substitute chicken liver for the beef liver. You could also restrict your carbohydrate intake over the course of a day and thereby develop a "free quota" you can use at dinner, or only eat half a serving.

Or you can do what I do and eat your English fried liver with a good conscience – you need to live a little!

Instructions:
- I fry the bacon and onions and put it aside.
- Then I brown the liver in the same pan. When it has the same colour on both sides, I put the bacon and onions back in the pan.

– I season with Dijon mustard and capers. Perhaps a dash of vinegar. Then I let it simmer for a few minutes.

A normal portion of this exclusive dish contains 600 kcal and 16 (!) g carbohydrates. Fat burning quotient: 0.45. I suggest that you consume these carbohydrates with good conscience. We should eat liver regularly, and we might as well eat it in the best possible manner!

Tomato and onion salad

I really enjoy tomato and onion salad, preferably with equal parts of tomatoes and onions. This is not an ideal dish for the GI-Zero! program since both tomatoes and onions contain large amounts of carbohydrates. A very small 100 g (3.5 oz) salad contains 5 g carbohydrates.

However, once in a while I eat this salad. It is particularly good with my cheese-filled meat dishes, and with small servings it is possible to stay under the 9 g carbohydrates limit.

The classic recipe:
1. Rub a salad bowl with a garlic clove or two.
2. Slice the tomatoes thinly and put them in the bowl.
3. Slice the onions thinly and scatter the rings over the tomatoes.
4. Sprinkle with French dressing (I also add some coarsely ground pepper).
5. Refrigerate.

A small portion of this salad contains 5 g carbohydrates. Fat burning quotient: 0.8.

Five minute salmon lunch

I want to remind you that you can fry cold-smoked salmon in a frying pan. Sauté the salmon together with some spinach or something else and add 100 g (3.5 oz) crème fraîche. Reduce and pepper to taste.

A good serving provides 600 kcal and 5 g carbohydrates. Fat burning quotient: 1.7. In this case, I have included spinach as a side dish. If you choose another vegetable, you will have an additional gram of carbohydrates.

Kebabs that everyone likes

Small metal skewers that work well in frying pans are available. With these you can make nutritional meals that are popular with all age groups, children included. If you serve kebabs with coleslaw, you are guaranteed success!

Instructions:

1. Make a large batch of coleslaw, preferably the day before.
2. Buy meat and bacon of different types, well-spiced sausage, plus bell pepper, champignon, and onions. There is nothing to stop you from using liver or kidneys. Cut the meat in chunks and blanch the vegetables.
3. Prepare a marinade of oil and lemon juice. Season to taste. I usually use garlic and Dijon mustard.
4. Mix the meat, bacon, and sausage with one or more vegetables. Put it on the skewer. A piece of bell pepper, a champignon, and a few chunks of onion are enough on each skewer.
5. Place the skewers in the marinade for 4–5 hours. It is easiest to marinade them in a plastic bag.
6. Fry the skewers in a hot pan. Serve with coleslaw.

A tightly packed skewer comes to 400 kcal and 5 carbohydrates. Fat burning quotient: 0.9. With a portion of coleslaw you will have 550 kcal and 8.7 carbohydrates. Fat burning quotient: 1.

Eating according to the GI-Zero! program

You need fat in your diet

Blood sugar levels that go up and down like a lift are a serious threat. They affect our health and lead to lack of energy. If you provide your body with fuel in the form of sugar, you must offer it a continual supply – this can be fruit, chocolate biscuits, or a cake with your coffee. Without regular injections of sugar you have trouble coping with lengthy physical exertions. When your blood sugar levels drop, you become tired and have trouble concentrating.

By practicing THE SCANDINAVIAN DIET you avoid these problems. Your blood sugar levels stabilise, making it easier for you to stay active. Your head clears, and you can't understand what is wrong with your colleagues. It is hard to remember that you were just like them only a few weeks ago.

Everyone should experience the health and mood improvements associated with a natural diet. However, you must turn a deaf ear to all the dumb messages we get from our authorities. A short time ago I heard a professor say that fat makes people stupid. She had come to this conclusion by feeding rats more fat than they are designed to eat!

Let us take a closer look at her "armchair" theory. Traditional hunters eat little sugar, and they eat lots of fat. Inuits, according to that professor's theory, should be especially thick.

They are, however, sharp enough to survive the daily threats of starving polar bears and short-tempered, surly walruses!

After a few weeks on THE SCANDINAVIAN DIET you will find out if you function like a rat or a human.

What do we need besides food?

If you endeavour to have a varied diet based on animal foods, you don't need any dietary supplements. Vegetable eaters have to take supplements or they will die. None of us eats as varied a diet as we should. And the animal foods that we eat are often of low quality. Meat should come from animals that mature on grass, but such products are not often available.

When I first started eating according to the GI-Zero! program, I had trouble with cramps in my legs and tried different dietary supplements. I can remember that calcium and magnesium helped. Or perhaps the cramps disappeared on their own. Sometimes, when I eat very restrictively and consume no carbohydrates in the course of a day, I can get leg cramps after a few days. The cramps are not at all as bothersome as they once were, and the problem disappears quickly. If I have supplements in the house, I take some. If not, I just wait. I let my body deal with the electrolyte balance on its own.

Under normal circumstances, I don't take any dietary supplements. I eat a varied diet of animal foods and trust that this food keeps me as healthy as it does the Inuits. The tests I take indicate that this is the case. However, it must be pointed out that my metabolism is completely different from a sugar eater, and that normal reference values can't be applied to someone on the GI-Zero! program.

There is a lot of controversy about vitamin C. When you want to explain the effects of the Inuit diet, you have a problem with vitamin C. A lot of effort has been spent trying to track down possible sources of vitamin C and finding them in the diet of mice and the stomachs and adrenalin glands of reindeer. I believe the solution is much simpler: a real fat eater doesn't need as much vitamin C as others!

Previously, I took several grams of vitamin C every day; today, I often consume less than the recommended daily intake. This works remarkably well. I am never sick, I have an extremely low level of oxidative stress, and I have the energy of a 25 year old. This started as an experiment, but I plan to continue in this manner. If I develop scurvy, I will let you know.

You can live on cheese alone

You can actually live quite well on cheese and water alone. Or just eggs and water. Normal fat cheese has almost ideal proportions of fat and protein. For example, a white mould cheese contains an energy percent of 75% fat and 25% protein. Normal brie has a relationship between fat and other nutrients of 1:33. With this relationship, it is difficult to store fat.

Suppose that you decide to live on a pound of brie per day. The cheese supplies 1670 kcal, and that is enough energy to live on. You would have 140 g fat, 105 g protein, and 1 g carbohydrates. Fat burning quotient: 1.3.

On a diet of brie you consume plenty of saturated fat. Most of your needs for vitamins and minerals are satisfied. This is easy to understand, since babies live exclusively on milk!

The only vitamin that is absent is vitamin C. The cheese also only contains 250 g water. Therefore, you should supplement your cheese diet with vitamin pills and a few litres of water. You could probably live on this diet for years without problems.

Cheese is a rescue buoy for many who need to eat something nutritional quickly. But it can also be a pitfall for some. A few of my students have reported that cheese prevented them from losing weight. When they dropped the cheese, their fat metabolism increased.

Why it is like this, nobody knows. It may be due to the fact that the milk proteins in cheese cause insulin release in certain sensitive individuals. Some recent research actually supports that interpretation. As you know, even a modest release of insulin reduces the metabolism of fat.

You can live on egg alone

Twenty eggs provide the same result, but offer a better suite of vitamins. Eggs constitute a high protein diet with a more modest intake of fat. The fat burning quotient stops at 0.76. This is also a good diet, but not as conducive to weight loss for the extremely overweight (a person who is less overweight will often show good progress on a high protein diet).

You must supplement an egg diet with a few litres of water and some vitamins. I would take vitamins C and D. You wouldn't notice any deficiencies during the first years.

In GI-Zero! you can eat as many eggs as you like. You will have excellent cholesterol values and low levels of triglycerides. If your health is poor, your total cholesterol may increase in the beginning. This actually means that the repair process is underway. When your arteries have formed stable cell walls, your total cholesterol will drop, and you will be at less risk of developing cardiovascular diseases.

In truth, cholesterol is not so dangerous; it is the body's most important repair material. The body has many mechanisms to form this critical substance. If you decrease your intake of cholesterol your body will increase its own production. That shows how important cholesterol is.

The American scientist and fraud Ancel Key laid the

foundation for our fear of cholesterol over fifty years ago. To this day, nutritional authorities in the Western world base their warning against cholesterol and saturated fat on his work.

But Ancel Key knew that you could eat as much cholesterol as you wanted. Towards the end of his career he revealed the truth:

"There is no relationship whatsoever between the cholesterol we eat and the amount of cholesterol in our blood. We have known this all the time. Only chickens and rabbits need to worry about their intake of cholesterol."

The damaging effects of cholesterol have actually only been investigated in chickens and rodents. These animals are vegetarians and have no tolerance for animal fat. But the nutritional authorities usually neglect to mention that fact when they refer to this research.

No need to worry about salt

If we are healthy, we don't need to concern ourselves about salt intake either. We get the salt that we need from our animal food. We don't risk any salt deficiency. If we eat too much salt, our bodies dispose of it naturally. Quite another thing is that the majority of my students report that sensitivity to salt increases on this diet. Suddenly bacon starts to leave a salty taste in the mouth. At this point, it is advisable to use fresh or lightly salted pork instead. This is actually positive, since bacon contains far too many additives and preservatives.

When should we eat?

When should we eat what we have decided to eat? Should we eat at regular intervals, or should we eat only when we are hungry? Should we eat breakfast? How useful or harmful are snacks between meals?

I have a fairly uncomplicated relationship to when I should

eat. I eat when my body wants food. A certain amount of regularity ensues based on that alone. Often I eat in the morning, in the afternoon, and in the evening. I can skip breakfast or lunch, but I never miss my evening meal. Snacks between meals are unnecessary in the GI-Zero! program.

We really aren't designed to eat breakfast, but disregard that for a moment. A normal person, who uses sugar as their fuel, needs food all the time. Primitive people didn't have pantries or refrigerators. Man has lived under these conditions for 99.9% of human history. The idea of cultivating the soil and storing food in cellars or pantries is a relatively recent invention.

Primitive people huddled in their caves until hunger forced them out to hunt for food. Perhaps they could catch a hare, check a trap, or dig up some bitter roots. If the season was right, they might gather a few handsful of hazelnuts. But lunch time came and went before there was food on the table, and thus primitive people never got fat. In fact, their biggest problem was storing enough fat on their bodies to survive the winter.

Your problem is just the opposite. You have regular access to foods that encourage fat storage, and you have no problem storing fat for the winter. The risk is rather that you continue to store fat throughout the winter, and are struck with fear when the next swimsuit season approaches …

Should we drop breakfast?

No, I don't think so. However, I do think that we should change our breakfast habits and stop eating food that, from the morning on, set the body in fat storage mode. Our first and most important step should therefore be to start the day with nutritional food, the same kind of food that we eat the rest of the day.

I commonly start the day with leftovers from a previous

dinner. I always prepare more food than I can eat, and so I usually have four or five tempting leftovers sitting in my refrigerator. This can be anything from leftover cheese souf-flé, which tastes fantastic reheated, to cheese-stuffed minute steaks or leftover grilled chicken. Cold chicken and mayon-naise is delicious! At the very least I can always fry some ham and eggs or eat a tin of mackerel in tomato sauce with a hardboiled egg. I always have hardboiled eggs in the refrig-erator. Or I make an omelette, see page 37.

"I have trouble with warm, prepared food in the morn-ing," say a few of my students. But after a few months this is no longer an issue. The body and your tastes adjust more quickly than you would think. Your present breakfast is nothing more than a habit. We eat an unnatural breakfast, and have similar dilemmas with our health. THE SCANDI-NAVIAN DIET re-educates and re-directs us to a more natural diet.

What happens when we eat according to GI-Zero!?

GI-Zero! is a program for health. When you start GI-Zero! you have started on a journey towards a new life. You will become healthier and stronger. A multitude of ailments will disappear, and you will sleep better at night. You will awaken refreshed and full of energy, and avoid periods of fatigue during the day.

With GI-Zero! you stop living life with limits and delays. Your new active body refuses to drag a mass of unnecessary fat around, and starts to normalise your weight. If you weigh too much, you lose weight; if you weigh too little, you gain weight. If you weigh what you should weigh, you replace fat with muscle.

The transition to GI-Zero! occurs in three phases. The first week you empty your sugar storage and begin a transi-tion to a ketone-based metabolism. It is possible you will feel unwell from day three until day six. Then the brain changes from sugar mode to ketone mode. Some become euphoric. This process is quite similar to the process you undergo when you fast. The difference is that you are eating until you are satisfied. In the course of a week or two these problems disappear, and you will feel better with each passing day.

Phase two lasts for a few months. Now the ketone-based metabolism is in full operation. You can measure its intensity with the help of so-called ketosis sticks. At the same time your body also gradually adapts to using fat as fuel.

In phase three you run your body and parts of your brain on fat. The adaptation to phase three occurs gradually over the course of the first six months. The need for carbohydrates disappears, and you can reduce your intake of protein. A fat-operated body needs very little dietary supplements to function optimally. I started phase three after about four months, and now I have managed my body on natural foods for six years. I am 65 years old, but I get stronger and more energetic each day. And in the course of those six years I haven't been sick once.

A little about ketosis

Many nutritional experts believe that we get more energy by eating carbohydrates. They think that strength as well as endurance decreases if you don't eat sugar. However, just the opposite is true: if you eat natural foods, you gain natural vitality.

The brain quickly adapts to ketone operation. The process takes less than two weeks. The physical adaptation takes much longer. Allow a few months for your strength and endurance to improve. After that you will beat all your previous records.

If you are active in endurance sports, you will find that

your energy levels increase greatly on GI-Zero! You can participate in all the marathons you want without other fuel than water. You have free access to your fat reserves. You live just like your ancestors did during periods of little food. People then needed an abundance of strength and endurance. If primitive man had become weak and dull due to lack of sugar, he wouldn't have survived.

There are many advantages associated with not using sugar as fuel; one of them is that your endurance increases. When we allow our body direct access to our own body fat, we have nutrition that lasts for weeks on end.

Don't follow the advice of nutritional experts!

Now you know what you should eat. If you want to know what you shouldn't eat, you can study the official nutritional recommendations. They recommend a diet not dissimilar to the one used to fatten animals prior to butchering. You must eat lots of carbohydrates and eat bread at every meal. This works well for perhaps half of the population, those who are underweight. The other half pays the price.

The situation is simple. Today's nutritional recommendations include an unnatural amount of easily digestible carbohydrates. At the same time they exhibit an unnatural lack of the natural fats that humans are designed to eat. If you eat like the authorities advise you to, you get sick. Sooner or later. Modern nutritional politics and dietary recommendations are responsible for the declining health of the population. This is a tragedy for most people, but a gold mine for the pharmaceutical industry.

Today, surgeons remove sections of the stomach of people who eat the wrong kinds of food, dramatically reducing their eating. The problem, however, is not the eating; the problem is that they are eating what the nutritional experts recommend. They should instead surgically insert a filter that prevents the dangerous foods, bread, and margarine from reaching the stomach. This would actually work better.

Depressing? Yes, but only for those who follow dietary recommendations! If you return to the food that you are designed to eat, you will regain your health. I am a living example of this.

I learned from a brown bear

Over the last six years, I have eaten a stone age diet similar to the diet of our primitive ancestors. Our primitive ancestors ate like the brown bear, accumulating fat with the help of sugar and easily digestible starches in the summer, and using that fat to help him survive the winter in his den.

We have the same ability as the bear to store fat, and then to live on it in lean times. The bear uses blueberries to build up his fat reserves; we use sugar and starch. The problem is that we have forgotten the reason for this fat storage. It is supposed to help us survive the winter, but today we eat to store fat all year around.

THE SCANDINAVIAN DIET breaks this pattern. You start to eat the "winter diet" of primitive man, the diet that we are designed to eat in lean times. By reducing the proportion of carbohydrates and increasing the proportion of fat you get two different menus. You eat via your mouth, and you eat from your reserves. You eat yourself to weight loss!

This has nothing to do with the concept of energy. Man is not a machine. Primitive man alternated between fat storage and fat burning, and I do too. I consciously increase my weight at least once a year. I do that to imitate our original life-style. But I keep the sugar-saturated period very short and the fat-eating period longer. It is my hormonal method for natural weight regulation and superior health.

This is the advanced course of THE SCANDINAVIAN DIET. Your first goal is to lose weight, not to live like primitive man. You should lose at least half of the weight you need to lose before you deviate from your fat-burning "winter diet".

If you have 4 stone (25 kg) or less to lose, you should go straight for your goal. If we're talking about 8 (50 kg) or 16 stone (100 kg) of excess weight, you should consider short periods with "summer food" once a year. This was the technique I used to get past weight loss "plateaus".

Living on the "winter diet" should not be a form of starvation. We can starve ourselves to weight loss, but we can't starve ourselves to good health. We are created to have optimal health and a properly functioning body. We can't achieve this through lack of food. If we do, we'll end up with a poorly functioning machine. The goal is a machine that functions better, a machine that burns all the fuel it takes in, and at the same time produces large amounts of energy and abundant good health.

Modern Western dietary recommendations encourage us to operate our bodies on nutrient-free energy (carbohydrates). This is advice for physical labourers, not for office workers. If we follow this advice, we become both fat and sick. We are overfed and undernourished at the same time!

What can we learn from history?

According to a well-known saying, "History teaches us that we have nothing to learn from history." This is particularly applicable to the history of dieting. There we find all we need to know, and even so we have determined to do exactly the opposite.

The great physician of antiquity, Hippocrates, offered two suggestions for weight loss: never perform strenuous labour on a fasting heart, and always eat fatty food, because small portions satisfy your hunger. This is simple advice that rings true even today.

The first example of GI-Zero!

One of the world's most famous food authors is the Frenchman Jean Anthelme Brillat-Savarin. His book *The Physiology of Taste* was published in 1826 and is a bible for all food lovers. Let us see what he had to say about the rise of obesity and its cure!

"Obesity will always be primarily caused by a diet overloaded with flour and starch."

The author provides many examples of this and states, "Animals that live on starchy food, by their own free will or not, become fat. This law also applies to man." And so a little addition: "Floury food works still quicker and more certain in combination with sugar."

What do we do to cure obesity? On this, Brillat-Savarin

is clear: "Since it has been shown that fat formation, in man as well as animals, can be attributed exclusively to floury and starchy food (…) it can be correctly concluded that a more or less strict abstinence from everything known as floury and starchy food must lead to a decrease in obesity."

So simple and so clear – and this was said 180 years ago!

Two people named William

Modern dieting developed between from 1860 and 1960. All the great discoveries were made during this time. Since then, the medical profession has spent the last forty years keeping the lid on it – often by explaining that the old knowledge doesn't exist!

William Harvey was an English ear doctor active in the mid-19th century. He advanced the theory that obesity and diabetes might have the same cause. If a pure animal diet was effective in controlling diabetes, a diet based on a combination of animal products and vegetables that didn't contain sugar or starch could be used to stop extreme fat formation. It was a revolutionary concept, and in the beginning of the 1860's Harvey got an opportunity to test his idea.

The test candidate was a wealthy businessman named William Banting. Harvey placed him on a diet that primarily consisted of meat and fat, with few carbohydrates. The results far exceeded both Harvey's and Banting's expectations, and thus the foundation for the first effective method of weight loss was established.

William Banting was an exemplary student. He had tried all known diets and cures, but only gained weight. Finally, he received advice that worked. He did further work on Harvey's basic idea and eventually formulated a simple guideline: "Eat until satisfied on meat and fat. Avoid bread, sugar, and potatoes. Then you will lose weight, even without exercise."

This is an exact description of THE SCANDINAVIAN DIET. But has the weight loss industry learned anything from William Banting and his success story? Is there anything about how we diet today that reminds us of this pioneer? Banting's original guidelines, *Letter on Corpulence,* are available on the internet today*.

Weight loss by German direction

My library contains *Corpulence and its treatment on physiological principles* by Wilhelm Ebstein, published in 1883. Ebstein was a Professor of Medicine in Göttingen, Germany, and one most influential doctors of his time. Here we find GI-Zero! again.

Like his predecessors, Ebstein states that fat people can be compared to fattened calves, and he cites carbohydrates as the decisive factor. If the goal is to reduce weight, then it is necessary to do the opposite of these fattened individuals. "The butcher's dog that eats meat and fat, never gets fat," said Ebstein. "But the lapdog becomes fat and lush on carbohydrates."

Ebstein put little faith in short-term cures, but recommended a permanent life-style change. Meat and fat should form the basis. "Of meat sorts I forbid none. I let the patient not avoid, but instead seek fat in meat. Sauces shall be prepared fat, and vegetables should be cooked in butter." He continues, "So-called 'starvation cures' are highly objectionable." Ebstein asserts that they only lead to greater fat storage.

Ebstein also points out that fat has two advantages when it comes to diabetes. It works against obesity, and ensures a slower digestion of food. Dietary fat is therefore "of great importance for the corpulent, who can be termed candidates for diabetes".

* www.lowcarb.ca/corpulence

A revolutionary experiment

Until recently there existed only a single definitive study of an animal-based diet and its effect on health. This study was conducted in the 1920's in Bellevue Hospital in New York. The world's leading scientists were involved, and the goal was to show, once and for all, what kind of food humans should eat.

For one year, two people, Vilhjalmur Stefansson and his colleague Karsten Anderson, lived on a diet completely lacking in fruit and vegetables. Instead they ate as much meat and fat as they wanted. The result shocked the scientific community. Both individuals maintained excellent health throughout the entire experiment. In fact, they improved their health!

Hardly anyone refers to this study today, but you can find it on the internet. The subjects of the experiment ate themselves to health on a diet that is considered unhealthy, and therefore the results did not lead to further research. Therefore, we who are interested must perform this research on our own. THE SCANDINAVIAN DIET is the result of such research.

A Swedish pioneer

One of the twentieth century's leading Swedish food writers was Pernilla Tunberger. Throughout a long and influential career, she recommended:

1. Vigilantly avoid bread, sweets, desserts, and fruit. Do not eat macaroons, spaghetti, or other flour products. They contain carbohydrates, and carbohydrates are the body's number one enemy in relation to being overweight. Also

watch out for carbohydrates in vegetables. Potatoes are the worst.

2. Other foods that should be avoided are brown beans, pea soup, and bananas. You should also be careful with beetroot, carrots, Jerusalem artichokes, peas, swedes, and parsnips.
3. If you want to lose weight, you must increase your metabolism by eating more meat, fish, eggs, and cheese. You should not fear fat, but avoid carbohydrates like the plague.
4. The major point of this system is that you can lose weight without hunger.

This is a brilliant summary. The author also points out the dangers that fruit poses for weight loss. It is good advice, since fruit turns off the metabolism of fat in carbohydrate-sensitive individuals.

Time of complications

During the twentieth century, many silly ideas about weight loss appeared; everything from dieting with alcohol to chewing your food for hours on end. One of the least successful methods was based on the idea that people function like ovens, and that you can control weight by counting calories. If you consume less energy than you metabolise, you lose weight. In theory it is correct, but it seldom functions in practice. The problem is that people don't like to be hungry. Sooner or later they start to eat again; they regain the pounds that they lost.

What we need is a model that allows people to lose weight and maintain that new weight for the rest of their lives.

At the moment we are in a depression. In addition to the calorie models, we have imaginative GI-models where you can eat all possible fat-forming food as long as it says "whole wheat" on the package. Sure, it would be great if we could eat low glycemic sweet rolls, desserts, and fruit and at the same time lose weight radically! But history tells us that this recipe does not work.

What can we learn from Sumo wrestlers?

When we study the regulation of weight, it is actually interesting to take a look at weight gain as well as weight loss.

If you want progress in your weight reduction, you can use THE SCANDINAVIAN DIET and send fat burning signals to your body. If, for some reason, you want to dramatically gain weight, then you do the exact opposite. But you have a difficult journey ahead.

It is actually quite difficult to gain extremely large amounts of weight. An old yo-yo dieter can do it, but for most people it is almost impossible. Most of us can gain one to three stone (13–19 kg) without difficulty, but if we want to gain 8 more stone (50 kg) our bodies say stop.

In a few cultures, it is considered attractive to be fat. Here we find the real weight gainers. Their recipe builds on the same hormonal basis, and usually includes a large proportion of carbohydrates and little fat.

The most effective weight-gainers can be found in the ancient Sumo culture in Japan. There they have practised weight gain for hundreds of years. You have to have a substantial body weight to toss a 31 stone (200 kg) opponent out of the ring. For Sumo wrestlers, it is important to gain weight rapidly at the start of their career. When they approach the top, they can use more time to build muscles.

A quick introduction to fat storage

In the southern part of Nigeria, live the Annang, a cultural and ethnic group where the aristocracy lock their daughters in special rooms to fatten them. Here the young girls are forced to sit still and eat millet porridge and milk before they are advertised on the marriage market – the fatter the bride, the higher the price. Carbohydrates have always formed the basis for this process, never meat and fat. Meat and fat were reserved for young warriors who weren't supposed to be fat.

On the islands in the South Pacific, taro and breadfruit function in the same way. The Japanese Sumo wrestler's recipe is "chanko". This is a lean meat and fish casserole with large amounts of rice. Large amounts of beer accompany the food. Rice and beer provide the necessary fat storage signals, and then they take a nap.

The low fat and carbohydrate-rich food provides little satisfaction and the Sumo wrestler is soon hungry again. This also helps them eat more. They exercise hard, but no exercise can eliminate so many carbohydrates. Therefore these fantastic athletes are also world champions in weight gain.

I have done a lot of investigation into the Sumo diet. The diet can vary a little, depending on a goal of weight gain or increase in strength. Aspirants in the lower classes easily eat 5000 kcal daily, with 12–14 percent energy from protein, about the same from fat, and 75 percent energy from carbohydrates. This is absolutely fantastic for gaining weight.

The highest class doesn't have the same need to gain weight. They often emphasise getting more energy and much more protein in their diet. Their fat intake is almost doubled, but still quite low. They don't want to lose weight! The master group that I analysed ate on average 5500 kcal, with 29 percent protein energy, 16 percent fat energy, and 55 percent carbohydrate energy.

The principle is simple. When you want to gain weight quickly, your diet must contain a large amount of carbohydrates. But when you reach the elite levels and need more muscle, you must eat substantially more protein. There is probably a limit to how fat you can become before you lose too much mobility. If you have seen Sumo wrestlers in action, you know that they are amazingly quick in relation to their body size.

Five thousand calories may not seem much, but the 75 percent energy is what does the trick. That is actually 10–15 percent more than Western nutritional authorities recommend in their carbohydrate-rich diet.

A match weight of 45 stone (286 kg)

The greatest Sumo wrestler of all was Konishiki. In his prime, he ate ten bowls of chanko, 8 giant bowls of rice, 130 pieces of sushi, and substantial amounts of grilled steak daily. Then came dessert. On this diet he went from a stable start weight of 27 stone (170 kg) to a "trimmed" match weight of 45 stone (286 kg).

Now Konishiki has retired and reduced his weight to about 39 stone (250 kg) – his wife weighs 32 stone less (200 kg)! He has lost weight on a low calorie chanko. You can lose weight on high carbohydrate food if you eat fewer calories, but Konishiki's results don't impress me. With THE SCANDINAVIAN DIET he would have lost 16 stone (100 kg) quickly!

I have studied the classic chanko recipes. They don't contain any magic ingredients, and are similar to the lean meat and vegetable casseroles in, for example, Weight Watchers. The point is to eat many portions and a lot of rice.

A Sumo wrestler eats twice as much as a regular Japanese

person. To achieve this food consumption he skims the fat off his pot of chanko several times. Otherwise he couldn't eat enough. If he leaves the fat, it would be hard to eat enough rice, and then his fat storage would be hindered.

You can exercise to gain stomach fat!

When you want to affect your body shape and re-distribute weight, it is important to combine diet and exercise correctly. Sumo wrestlers exercise hard and long on empty stomachs. This shows that exercise is no help when the diet is wrong. They work up a good appetite, stress their body, and increase their cortisone levels. In this manner they also lay a foundation for gaining proper stomach fat. A successful wrestler has to have a low centre of gravity! Then they eat much more than they should in one meal and take a nap. That is another good recipe for weight gain.

The low fat Sumo diet provides all the components that a successful weight gainer needs. Unfortunately, the diet does have negative effects on health. Most Sumo wrestlers develop diabetes and die early. The plate mode can have this effect!

"The soul sits in the stomach."
Old Japanese proverb

What can we learn from the brown bear?

The brown bear is a perfect illustration of how an overweight person functions. We really don't need any diet books. We should just study brown bears.

The brown bear is a predatory meat and plant eater, just like humans. It achieves optimal strength and health on a meat-based diet, just like humans. It uses carbohydrates, primarily blueberries, to gain fat, just like humans.

The brown bear can easily use fat as a source of nutrients, in the same way humans do. But when the bear eats blueberries, it stops burning fat because the carbohydrates turn off fat burning – that applies to both bears and humans. There are, of course, people who can eat unlimited amounts of carbohydrates and not gain a gram – but these people won't be reading this book!

The brown bear practises hormonally controlled weight gain. It eats sugar, sugar, and more sugar. With the help of sugar (blueberries) the bear blocks fat burning and manages to increase body weight by a third over a few months. The bear is actually a better yo-yo dieter than any human.

Brown bears are eminent berry pickers. According to the Swedish Hunters' Association, bears in North America consume a third of their own weight in berries per day in the autumn. A bear that weighed 50 stone (315 kg), ate 184 000 berries in the course of a day. Try to keep up with a bear when it comes to picking berries!

184 000 blueberries weigh 14 stone 7 (92 kg) if each berry weighs 0.5 g. That corresponds to 42 500 kcal and 8400 g carbohydrates. Fat burning quotient: 0.07. (A fat burning quotient of 0.1 is an excellent weight gain diet. This is in keeping with what Western nutritional authorities and specialists recommend. You have to eat starvation rations to maintain your weight with such a fat burning quotient – but the bear isn't eating starvation rations at all!)

If the brown bear made the mistake of killing a moose or two in the autumn, and ignored the blueberries, it would die during hibernation. It would freeze and starve to death. It is quite impossible to build up necessary fat reserves based on animal foods alone. Carbohydrates are absolutely necessary. This is the reason why THE SCANDINAVIAN DIET contains so much animal food and so few carbohydrates.

One doctor contributed the following to the debate:

1. What does a bear eat in the spring? Yes, exactly, meat, fish, eggs, and fat. Bears don't eat carbohydrates in the spring. They stay slender and vigorous, and have the strength to mate.
2. What do bears eat in the autumn to increase their weight for the winter hibernation? In the autumn it is berries, fruit and grass.
3. What kind of food do the Western nutritional authorities recommend for losing weight? Just what the bear eats to gain weight! I think that bears are smarter than Western nutritional authorities.

Björn Hammarskjöld, Paediatrician,
PhD in Biochemistry

Food and health

This is a very sensitive chapter that will probably infuriate many doctors. But I'm writing it anyway. Thousands of people have written to me and shared their miraculous progress to health and improved quality of life. I experienced the same. It would be wrong of me not to provide a short summary of their experiences as well as mine.

After six years on this diet, I can safely say that THE SCANDINAVIAN DIET is a certain road to superior health. You can count on reducing your weight and improving your diabetes, high blood pressure, and all kinds of joint and skin problems. The irritated bowel will have an opportunity to heal, your allergies will diminish, and your general quality of life will improve.

Many hormonal problems will decrease or disappear. If you suffer from menstruation pain, polycystic ovary syndrome (PCOS), or infertility, THE SCANDINAVIAN DIET may help. I have many thank-you letters from people who have experienced considerable health benefits.

Even if you don't regard yourself as sick today, you will notice large changes. Like most people, you have forgotten how it feels to be truly healthy.

Food as medicine

In the health profession, great effort is expended on treating different deficiencies and ailments. The focus is the body's infirmities, while THE SCANDINAVIAN DIET concentrates on the body's strengths, on its ability to heal itself.

THE SCANDINAVIAN DIET builds an immune system that can withstand most attacks. A bad cold will last perhaps half an hour; then the immune system goes into action.

THE SCANDINAVIAN DIET helps you to sleep quietly and peacefully and to tackle stress. You achieve an inner peace that withstands most onslaughts. Stress may develop, but it doesn't affect you in the same way as before. You form an immune system that tolerates stress!

Quite simply, it seems that a natural diet can deal with many of the problems that afflict us today. "Food should be your medicine", in the words of Hippocrates, the Father of Medicine.

I have received e-mails and telephone calls from over 5 000 people who eat according to my principles. Most claim weight reduction. EVERYONE experiences health benefits. The list of illnesses that have been cured or alleviated by this diet goes on and on.

Food that causes illnesses?

During the 20th century, there was a substantial increase in cardiovascular disease, diabetes, cancer, and strokes. A whole panorama of auto-immune and auto-aggressive illnesses appeared. This increase went hand-in-hand with an increased intake of processed agricultural products, covertly sugared and chemically-infused food, and artificially produced fat (margarine).

It is not scientifically proven that food is responsible for these ailments, but when people stop eating pre-fabricated food, they become healthy. Many report that their health has been restored after decades of suffering from various ailments and illnesses. A common statement is that they "have got their life back".

In the beginning, these reports on improved health surprised me. I had improved my own health, but I thought perhaps it was just me. However, it became apparent that everyone who ate this diet experienced similar health benefits.

What do the physicians say?

The most common comment I hear is that health improvement is due to weight loss, even though it is often the health benefits that cause the weight loss. The concept that diet alone can have such an effect on our health seems radical to many people. Doctors often threaten their patients with all the illnesses that will come if they don't immediately return to a more "balanced" diet.

Physicians are no dumber than other people, but they have often developed a narrow viewpoint. Their education is based on treatment through prescription drugs or surgery. That is what they consider "medicine". A doctor who treats serious illnesses with dietary changes will likely risk his license. The fact that his patients improve doesn't count.

I am no doctor and lack any form of medical education. Therefore, I can take the chance of saying what I want to say. After listening to several thousands of my students, I concluded that most of our illnesses are either due to, or become worse from, sugar. A high intake of sugar and the substances that quickly transform to sugar, leads to our being overweight and developing diabetes. It disturbs the intestinal flora, and it causes a wide variety of inflammatory conditions. High sugar consumption weakens the immune system, and makes cancer cells grow unrestrained.

This is not the opinion of science; it is my own opinion. If we maintain low, stable blood sugar levels, we stop or cure the illnesses that are afflicting us.

Take my own case

We can deal with negative, distorted life-styles for many years, but sooner or later our bodies protest. I ate a lot of bread, pasta and polenta for fifty years. I used margarine instead of butter, and I lived with constant high blood pressure and constant high insulin levels. Finally, my body went on strike.

A doctor told me that I weighed 11 stone (70 kg) too much, another that my blood pressure was the highest he had ever seen. One physician discovered heart failure, another pre-diabetes (an initial stage of diabetes). And all of them could see that my circulation was failing. I was not yet 60 years old, and my prognosis was dismal.

Today, I am healthier than all of these physicians. I am no longer overweight, and all of my other health problems have simply disappeared. At an age of 65, I am stronger and healthier than most 25 year olds. I have very low oxidative stress, and I don't need anti-oxidants. I am finished with a normal cold or the flu in less than an hour. My immune system conquers all.

However, this is a very subjective experience. How does my health look measured against the scientific standards? To find this out I visited physician Calle Carlsson and his laboratory. He runs a private health institution in Österäng in Sweden. Here he heals patients that the ordinary health services have abandoned. His method consists primarily of diet and life-style changes, not drugs. You can read more about Calle Carlsson later in the book.

Quite simply, I wanted to know how the food I ate affected my body. There is no point in losing weight if the diet kills you.

A fat eater's health

According to the Western nutritional authorities I should probably be dead, because I am doing everything wrong.

Here are some of my test results:

1. Liver function (different transaminases, or enzymes that allow transfer of amino groups) should lie between 0.0 and 0.70. I had 0.22 and 0.29.
2. Blood sugar levels after fasting should lie between 3 and 6. I had 4.3.
3. Total cholesterol should lie between 3.5 and 6.8. I had 5.4.
4. The "good" cholesterol (HDL) should lie between 0.8 and 2.1. I had 2.1.
5. The "bad" cholesterol (LDL) should lie under 4.0. I had 3.5.
6. C-reactive protein (CRP) is a modern sedimentation rate (ESR). Many consider this an important measure. It should lie between 0 and 20. I had 1.6.
7. Blood pressure was normal (134/81), blood value (hb) was 15.2. EKG was normal. No cancer indicators were found. No sign of kidney problems.

All in all, it looks like I am in excellent health. I don't think that there is a fat-frightened physician in the Western world with health as good as mine!

Everyone becomes healthy

I now receive reports from thousands of people who have the same experience, people who live as they are intended to live, manage to cure diabetes, irritated intestines, and infertility. They achieve better health, lose weight, and they no longer have to use insulin, statins, and blood pressure medicines. They avoid inflammation and pain, and regain mobility. Allergies of all kinds disappear or diminish, along with fibromyalgia and over-sensitivity. People avoid the surgical removal of parts of their intestine, and they avoid starvation diets. They keep their inner organs, and they don't need to live with a stigmatising bag on their stomach.

These are amazing medical achievements, but when I tell doctors about this, they say that I have to obtain scientific evidence. However, they don't tell me how I should do this. It costs a vast amount of money to perform a controlled scientific study – and such a study should ideally be conducted over many years. Only pharmaceutical companies can afford studies like this, and they aren't interested in studies of people who cure themselves without the benefit of drugs.

But even if nothing at all is happening on the research front, there are many doctors who are working in the quiet. They give their patients sensible dietary advice and they see rapid improvements. Åsa Larsson, from Trollhåttan in Sweden, is one of them. You can read more about her on page 215. This is what she has to say about triglycerides (triglycerides are a much more important measurement than cholesterol, and the values should be low):

"With a low carbohydrate diet, triglyceride values decline, sometimes to as much as a fifth of the initial value. This applies to all our patients who follow a low carbohydrate regime. We are now talking about hundreds of patients, so I know what I am talking about."

About a Polish doctor

I provide dietary advice to overweight, relatively healthy people. The seriously ill I refer to doctors. But sometimes I get reports about very serious cases where sick individuals fight a bitter battle against a life-threatening disease. This may be someone who, in accordance with their own beliefs, tries to starve their cancer cells by denying them sugar. This may seem like a strange idea, which they haven't gotten from me. My guess is that they read about the Polish physician Jan Kwasniewski.

Kwasniewski treats all kinds of illnesses with what he calls "Optimal Nutrition". This is exactly the same diet that I started on six years ago. Kwasniewski says that a cancer cell dies in the course of a few hours when placed in an egg yolk. In contrast, it grows uncontrolled when placed in a sugar solution. Therefore, he gives his patients a lot of egg yolks, but very little sugar. Any doctor who used this treatment in Sweden would lose his license.

Jan Kwasniewski also cures obesity, diabetes, heart problems, and many kinds of stomach and intestinal disorders. His experience is completely in agreement with my own.

If you want to know more about Jan Kwasniewski and his theories, his book "Optimal Nutrition" is published in both English and German. You should be aware that most doctors aren't familiar with Jan Kwasniewski. And even if they know who he is, they disagree with his conclusions. Let's take diabetes as an example. An ordinary Western doctor regards diabetes as a life-long illness that gradually worsens. It is a "natural progression" that can't be stopped, says the doctor. I know that is not true for type-2 diabetes. This "sickness" was formerly called "sugar sickness", and it can always be alleviated or cured. All that is required is that you remove sugar from your diet.

Type-1 diabetes is more difficult to treat, and I don't advise patients who suffer from it. Jan Kwasniewski says that it is possible to successfully treat Type-1 diabetes with dietary measures, but that is his own claim. Some people with Type-1 have written to me. They have been able to reduce their insulin medication, but none have been able to stop taking their medication completely. On the other hand, many people with adult-onset diabetes (type 2) have been able to throw away their medications after they started THE SCANDINAVIAN DIET.

Many people who have bought this book are looking for a weight loss program. If you belong to this group, you have made a good choice. You will lose weight. If you are very overweight, you will lose more weight with this program than any other. And you will never be hungry.

But the most fantastic aspect of THE SCANDINAVIAN DIET is not the weight loss; it is the phenomenal benefits to your health!

"The only exercise I get consists of following caskets with dead friends who lived as they had been told to live."

Peter O'Toole (75), according to *Expressen* (a Swedish newspaper).

THE SCANDINAVIAN DIET
and diabetes

"Sugar sickness", or type-2 diabetes, is a life-style disease. You develop it when you eat incorrectly and when you live incorrectly. People who eat a natural diet don't develop it. Diabetes is an acquired disease. We come by it from drinking sugar water (soda and juices) and eating sweet rolls baked with nutrient-free flour. Sugar sickness should really be called *carbohydrate sickness*. If we stop eating carbohydrates, we can free ourselves from this sickness that is a side-effect of the way we eat.

Curing type-2 diabetes is a simple task. It is much easier than curing extreme obesity. Even so, you seldom hear a physician talk about curing diabetes. That statement is not part of their vocabulary. I bet that they aren't even aware of the fact that diabetes can be cured.

Sweden's most successful diabetes doctor is Jörgen Vesti-Nielsen. He cures diabetes. Åsa Larsson in Trollhättan cures diabetes. And Annika Dahlqvist in Njurunda has sold almost 500 000 books on THE SCANDINAVIAN DIET and how to cure diabetes and other modern lifestyle illnesses. In Norway, physician and author Sofie Hexeberg has treated countless patients for a variety of ailments simply by changing their diet. (Both of these books will soon be available in English.)

Doctors who recommend that diabetics change their diet are persecuted and opposed by nutritional physiologists.

Curing diabetes does not comply with accepted science and practical experience. Diabetes is by definition an incurable disease, with a tragic and inexorable "natural progression". Curing diabetes is a crime against science!

Jörgen Vesti-Nielsen and his research team at Karlshamn in Sweden have received international attention, but in Sweden no one gives them the time of day. The research team presents long-term controls of diabetics who have been put on a moderate to low carbohydrate diet, a regime that is much more liberal than THE SCANDINAVIAN DIET. Even with this diet, they achieve results that are impossible with conventional treatment. They have recently reported the first cases of improvement in people with reduced kidney function! This is a medical sensation, but comments from the Swedish authorities are reserved. The result is not achieved with a patentable substance, and therefore the method is not interesting.

It is not only those who treat diabetes who lack interest in a natural cure. I have participated in several discussion groups for diabetics, and quite often I have been verbally abused. Diabetics are often dependent on sugar; otherwise, they wouldn't have developed diabetes, and some want to have their "incurable" illness in peace. People who might take away their sweet roll are regarded as threats.

I no longer participate in these forums. Below is what I wrote in a letter to decline further association:

"Well, I have noted that the majority of people in this forum prefer not to treat their diabetes in a natural manner by changing their diet. They apparently think that they have a 'right' to eat what their bodies can't tolerate. They should not be forced to live a more restrictive life than others just because they are sick. I can understand such a point of view, but fortunately those with an allergy to nuts don't think the same way.

I cure diabetics on many levels and joined this list as a

service to you. If you want to pull the plug, be my guest! Don't forget that although the medical profession wants to treat your sickness, they don't want you to get well!"

At the time, I was disturbed because I had recently written to several diabetes physicians and presented my method for a simple diabetes cure. None of them replied. That was a few years ago, and at that time I didn't understand that illness must be cured with drugs. And I definitely didn't understand that you can't cure "incurable" disease.

Below, I share with you my letter to the diabetes physicians. I promise that they have already had the opportunity to read the letter several times. I am determined that, in the end, all the adult-onset diabetics in the Western world will be informed that there is, in fact, a cure, even if their doctors refuse to acknowledge it.

The letter that no one wanted to answer

Hello, Tomas!

In the course of the last months, I have undeservedly become one Sweden's most successful people in the field of diabetic care. The background for this is that last summer I published a book on weight loss, where I recommend a fat-rich, animal-based diet. The book is primarily directed towards extremely overweight individuals who have trouble losing weight by conventional methods.

Naturally, I recognised that this must be a suitable diet for diabetics because it maintains stable levels of blood sugar, but I didn't write about this specifically in the book. Now the development has surprised me. A few months following the release of the book, diabetics started to send me reports and numbers that I didn't understand. The essence was that their blood sugar was in the process of normalising, and that they were able to reduce their medication. In addition, they lost weight.

A few months later, new accounts followed. I especially like the story about a physician who, wondering what has happened, listens to the patient describe his new diet, and replies that it certainly can't be due to the fat-rich diet …

As of today, at least 25 diabetics have been able to completely stop their medication, and just as many have been able to reduce their medication. It is apparent that most of them have changed their diet and reduced their medication on their own. They consider themselves competent to perform satisfactory measurements and they don't dare tell what they are doing when they go to the clinic. I would guess that there are also some undisclosed numbers here.

I have "cured" 25 diabetics in less than five months without being a doctor and without even trying. How many diabetics does a normal diabetes specialist cure in the course of a year? With his carbohydrate-rich recommendations? I bet he doesn't cure any. Most likely he claims that diabetes can't be cured.

As an amateur in your business I want only to register my dismay over the fact that Western diabetes specialists offer dietary recommendations that aggravate the prognosis of their patients, both in the short and long term. Which is what happens when you recommend a diet that causes a patient's blood sugar levels to rise.

I understand that you are in a kind of a network of diabetes specialists. Some with whom I correspond say that you are a bright person and that you recommend exercise as a solution. Which is why I am writing to you. Exercise is good, but you can never achieve results as beneficial as those you will achieve with dietary changes.

I know that they are taking steps in the right direction in Karlshamn, in Trollhättan too. But they need to go the full distance. Too many carbohydrates and much too little fat! And even the careful dietary changes they make there are being critisised. What must be done to get my way of eating introduced on a broad basis in the treatment of diabetes? Do you have any suggestions? Are you at all aware that it is possible to "cure" a long-term diabetic in a very short time with the help of a fat-rich and carbohydrate-free diet? Have you ever tried this with any of your patients?

Have you considered what the word "heal" really means? The way things are today, a majority of diabetes specialists recommend diets that causes diabetics' blood sugar to rise. In my ears this sounds grotesque, but it is the truth. Then they attempt to treat the consequences with medicine, perhaps in combination with exercise. Is this "healing"?

Sincerely,
Sten Sture Skaldeman

That was one of my letters. What answer do you think that I received? None whatsoever, of course. No diabetes specialist wants to hear that he can tear up his prescription pad and prescribe a new menu to his patients instead. That is not why he had such a long education.

The medical profession prefers sick patients!

There is a simple solution for your type-2 diabetes. Start THE SCANDINAVIAN DIET! But you must be strong enough to withstand the diabetes specialists and the diabetes associations who fiercely defend their livelihoods, and the economic benefits that follow from the actively prescribing of drugs. It is profitable for them that you continue to be sick!

Let me illustrate with a striking example. In March 2006, the Swedish national association of dieticians directed sharp criticism towards Jörgen Vesti-Nielsen's research project in Karlshamn, because it was in conflict with science and practical experience. At the association's annual meeting, they declared a researcher who had defected from the Karlshamn project to be "The Nutritional Specialist of the Year". The reason she received the award was that she had opposed (!) the research project in an exemplary manner.

My summary:

The dietary recommendations in the Western world for type-2 diabetics are based on carbohydrates and lack of scientific support. Those who follow these recommendations continue to be chained to their illness, while those who do the opposite can actually reduce or cease medication. If they return to the official dietary recommendations, their illness returns!

In Norway, there is a new association with broad expertise for diabetics and overweight people. The well-known nutritional physiologist Dag Viljen Poleszynski has led the effort to establish Society for Dietary Reform to Alleviate Diabetes (KOS)*.

"Kill me with poison rather than with sugar."
Arabic proverb

---

* A fast-growing Norwegian non-profit organisation working with physicians and activists to change the way we eat.

What does science have to say?

Am I a lonely screwball who doesn't know what he is talking about, or have I stumbled upon a natural and safe route to weight loss and good health? Who is telling the truth, me or our official nutritional authorities?

If you ask our established authorities, the ones who get bonuses from the food industry and pharmaceutical firms to say that the dietary recommendations are correct, they will say that the dietary recommendations are correct. The only response I get from them is silence. Thus far, no expert has dared to meet me in a debate.

However, if you ask smart doctors in active practice, those who work with fat and sick people on a daily basis, you can hear them say in informal situations that I am right and the experts are wrong.

I have contact with a large number of practising physicians who risk their careers by giving their patients health-promoting dietary advice. Many of them could have set up a GI-Zero! sign outside their offices. But they would risk losing their license. I don't intend to write about them; their efforts are best done behind the scene.

Others have risked telling the truth and have often had to pay a high price. Let's listen to some of these brave voices. In this chapter, I will write a few words about them and cite their articles. You will discover a striking similarity between their views and mine. This is completely natural, since these brave physicians express the truth. When the history of nutrition is one day written, these doctors will be standing with honour, while today's corrupt experts will stand with shame!

Calle Carlsson in Österäng

Calle Carlsson, a physician in Österäng, Sweden, is legendary. I only recently met him, and we quickly became good friends. To my surprise, I found in Calle a Swedish doctor who, for 25 years, has proclaimed dietary ideas that essentially agree with mine. It is a miracle that he still has his license.

Just like the others who tell the truth, he has had to pay a high price. His practice is outside the welfare system, and his patients have to pay the entire cost themselves. You don't get rich from such a practice. But Calle Carlsson and his wife Annika work hard in their private health institution. Their days are much longer than other people's. Their pay is modest, but their patients do get well.

Calle Carlsson was the first professional to come out with the GI concept. He was ahead of Montignac, and he was twenty years ahead of the businessmen who run weight clubs and sell GI-labelled products.

"We were not only first out, what we offer is better," says Calle Carlsson. "This applies especially to diabetes patients. They come in like corpses and undergo fantastic improvements in just 14 days. The explanation is not mega-doses of drugs, but the food we serve that improves blood sugar control.

It is not difficult to follow our program. Eat butter, meat, and cheese, be careful with carbohydrates, and let the unnatural, low-fat products remain on the store shelves!"

Frequently Asked Questions

Calle Carlsson was 20 years ahead of GI-Zero!
Here are some frequently asked questions:

– Is fat tantamount to high GI-values?
Answer: "No, on the contrary. Fatty foods are at zero GI. A lot of people have been successful in radically reducing their blood sugar by eating mostly fatty foods and by gradually lowering their carbohydrate intakes, that is, no potatoes or bread."

– Eggs have always been thought to cause high cholesterol, but you still recommend eggs.
How do you explain that?
Answer: "Eggs are one of the best foods we have – strictly fat and protein. GI-value 0. Eating 3 or 4 eggs per day is not a problem."

– You usually advise against eating potatoes.
Can't we ever allow ourselves a single potato?
Answer: "Of course you can if it's just once in a while. However, one exception tends to lead to another. The safest thing is to avoid them altogether. I myself eat natural rice or nothing at all with my fish or meat."

Continually opposed

Calle Carlsson is an expert at expressing himself dramatically, and he usually speaks his mind clearly:

"Shall we try to fix your leg with a correct diet, or shall we just saw it off?" he asks his patients.

Other doctors don't say things like that. With the best intentions, or for the sake of peace, most provide non-controversial advice that doesn't offend anyone. That the leg may end up amputated because of this advice is simply called "natural progression". But that progression is far from natural!

What does Calle Carlsson think about these preventable diseases?

"To get right to the point, I am willing to say that every heart attack and every case of adult-onset diabetes is, in principle, unnecessary. We eat and drink ourselves to these diseases."

Calle Carlsson has performed some 75 000 physical exams. He knows what he is talking about, and he is not above making bets with his patients.

Another Swedish truth teller

Björn Hammarskjöld is a paediatrician in Mora, Sweden, with a PhD in Biochemistry. Doctors who know their biochemistry usually don't believe the standard dietary recommendations for diabetics – they know too much chemistry for that. I found a review of one of Björn's articles, and here are some quotes:

"After exhaustive studies of the literature from the last century, we know that insulin is released when the blood's sugar content rises. Insulin forces sugar (glucose) into the cells, where the glucose joins and develops into long, complicated glucose chains called "glycogen". People can make about 0.5 kg glycogen," writes Hammarskjöld, "but insulin," he continues, "is an anabole, a body-building hormone. If the sugar content of the blood continues to be high – well, then the sugar surplus transforms instead into saturated fat. And we humans can store a hundred times – yes, a thousand times more fat than the 0.5 kg with glycogen."

He continues, "So the nutritional authorities, nutritional physiologists and the medical profession demand that diabetics should eat more carbohydrates to compensate for the increased amount of insulin that the nutritional authorities recommend, and so on, and so on in a vicious circle.

Our diabetics are almost always overweight or fat. And that is because they are forced to eat more carbohydrates than their metabolism is able to handle," asserts Hammarskjöld. "Therefore, they take insulin to reduce their blood sugar levels – which only increases fat storage. If their blood sugar drops too low, they need more carbohydrates, and the patient ends up in a negative cycle.

People have been hunters for more than 10 000 generations. Back then, they primarily lived on raw animal products. How much do our modern hunters, the Inuits and Saami, cultivate? Absolutely nothing. Instead they eat meat, fish, eggs and fat. And they aren't overweight and don't suffer from diabetes or cardiovascular disease.

This is usually explained as a paradox, at least by those who don't know any biochemistry. But it not a paradox. The truth is that we need meat and fat, but not a single sugar molecule at all."

Science versus reality

Åsa Larsson in Trollhättan, Sweden, is one of many doctors who have also arrived at principles similar to those with which I operate. I cite from an article in *Medicinsk Access*, number 1/2007:

"My cousin is in her seventies. Ten years ago, she developed type-2 diabetes. She weighed about 14 stone (90 kg) and took medication for hypertension (high blood pressure). Right from the start the doctor prescribed Metformin and statins (cholesterol lowering medicines) when they came into fashion, and she was given the usual advice about weight loss. After none of this helped, she heard about the influence of carbohydrates on body weight. She started to reduce her intake of carbohydrates and registered weight loss at once. In addition, she was able to reduce her medication.

For over two years, she has religiously followed my advice concerning carbohydrate reduction and increased fat intake. She has avoided light products and snacks between meals, and for two years she has weighed about 10 stone 3 (65 kg). She has discontinued diabetes medication and reduced the use of blood pressure medicines.

Not so long ago, she met her regular physician in the grocery store. He praised her for her weight loss and commented on her apparent good health. 'You have followed my advice, I see,' he said as they stood in the cash register line. 'No,' she answered, 'I have done exactly the opposite, eaten fat and cut out sugar, bread, pasta, and rice.'

She is only one of hundreds of patients in a project that we have worked on for two and a half years at Trollhättan. In this project, patients reduced their intake of carbohydrates and increased the amount of fat in their diet. Everyone who have followed these simple rules has lost weight, lowered their blood pressure, and reduced or discontinued their diabetes medication, including insulin.

Like the nutritional authorities, the public health institute and health authorities continue to claim that this doesn't work. Those of us who see these patients daily, know that it does. At the very least, we know that a large number of people, among them many doctors, who in some cases, have followed the program for as long as ten years, have lost weight and maintained their low weight.

While I have been writing this chapter, yet another of the many e-mails I have received has appeared in my inbox. This patient writes:

"I have now eaten fatty fish, eggs, cream, and butter in large amounts for a whole year and lost a large amount of weight, so I thought it best to visit my doctor and check my cholesterol levels. They had decreased quite a bit. The nurse couldn't understand it."

Åsa Larsson

A passionate soul speaks out

Annika Dahlqvist, a doctor in Sweden, has challenged the establishment. She has provided patients with dietary advice that has improved their health. She was the first public figure to recommend a Low Carb High Fat-diet, the diet we refer to in this book as THE SCANDINAVIAN DIET. Annika has a blog that has received a considerable amount of attention and she has sold almost 500 000 books in Scandinavia. I have selected a few quotes:

"I no longer eat any bread or other grain products, pasta, potatoes, rice, or sugar. I eat a lot of fat, primarily in the form of cream in my coffee, crème fraîche with food, full-fat sour cream, brie, avocado, fat meat and bacon. I have oil on vegetables. It has become a habit, and I don't think about it anymore."

"Of course, not everything depends on diet, but after I changed my diet from low fat-high carbohydrate to low carbohydrate-high fat, I never feel that life is depressing. I feel like life is incredibly exciting, and I experience a bubbling energy … I feel so marvelously healthy!

Often I receive similar blog comments about how people feel so good on this diet. Both in body and soul."

"During early human development people lived by hunting, fishing, and gathering of edible greens, roots, berries, and fruits. No human would have considered refusing the fat; it was a delicacy that provided energy, strength, and health!

Three major studies of populations: the Malmö study by Margret Leosdottir, the Uppsala study by Annika Smedman, and the North Sea project by Eva Warensjö, each showed individually and quite clearly that those who ate more dairy products, full of the dreaded saturated fat, had better cardio-vascular health.

With the knowledge that we have today, everything indicates that natural animal fats are good for your health, and that margarine and polyunsaturated oils damage health."

"While we wait for the proper scientific observations of what kind of distribution of fat, proteins, and carbohydrates achieve the best weight control and health, we should eat like our ancestors ate. To be specific, abundant saturated animal fat and very few carbohydrates!

I dare you to disprove my statements!"

Ralf Sundberg on cholesterol

When a doctor tries natural foods on his own body, some-times his eyes can be opened to the truth. This very thing happened to Ralf Sundberg in Malmö. After he had main-tained his new diet for several months, his patients started to wonder what had happened to the old doctor that they used to visit. But it was the same doctor, just in a new body. Ralf Sundberg writes:

"Do women with high cholesterol run a higher risk of heart attack? No, they don't. High cholesterol is not a risk factor for any disease in women. High cholesterol is actually a guarantee for a long and healthy life. Low cholesterol, on the other hand, indicates a shorter life span.

This is really not strange. Cholesterol is one of the body's most important substances. It is the most common organic molecule in the brain. Cholesterol stabilises our cell mem-branes. The hormones that regulate our fertility are built on this basic molecule.

Mother's milk contains saturated fat and cholesterol. Why, if cholesterol is so unhealthy? Why is a chicken egg so rich in cholesterol and saturated fat if they are such damaging substances? The answer, naturally, is that evolution, adapted us for natural foods and the natural substances our body needs.

Warm-blooded animals, like humans or chickens, produce saturated fat. When we eat a lot of polyunsaturated fat, the cholesterol level in our blood sinks because the walls of the cells start to leak, and because cholesterol is then taken from the blood to repair the cell walls. This registers as low cholesterol but no one is any healthier.

Increasing obesity is a problem, and the groundwork for it is laid early. The reason is too little intake of fat and a too high intake of sugar.

Saturated fat supposedly increases cholesterol. However, ten separate studies, where the carbohydrate content of food was reduced and patients were put on a diet with two to five times more saturated fat than the Western world's nutritional authorities recommend, show that cholesterol was not affected. In fact, a strong reduction in triglycerides – another risk factor was documented.

It is also claimed that saturated fat can lead to diabetes. However, all studies performed on diabetics where the amount of carbohydrates in the diet was reduced and replaced by more fat, especially saturated fat, resulted in a substantial improvement of the diabetes.

Another persistent myth is that you get fat from fat. A recent doctoral dissertation from Gothenburg showed that four-year-olds who ate less fat had a higher risk of developing obesity and diabetes, while those who ate the most fat were slender and healthy. This can seem like a paradox, but it is in complete agreement with what biochemistry and physiology say about our metabolism.

The scientific studies that support the opinion that milk fat is advantageous are quite well anchored in reality."

Ralf Sundberg, Doctor of Medicine.

The light dawns in Finland!

The following is reported by a Finnish biologist:

"Today I attended a very interesting defence of a doctoral dissertation at Åbo University, Sweden. At the Department for Biochemistry and Nutritional Chemistry, mag. art. Saska Tuomasykka was defending his dissertation *Strategies for reducing Postprandial Triacylglycerolemia*. His opponent was Professor Tom Sanders from King's College in London. Here are some of the conclusions:

1. The Health Institute's limits for fat are erroneous and should be corrected.
2. The national recommendations concerning our daily diet (Nordic Nutrition Recommendations 2004, plate model) are excellent for top athletes, but terribly bad for those who exercise less than athletes.
3. Insulin is the foremost villain in this drama, for together with the known effect that insulin has on carbohydrate metabolism, it also has a considerable influence on the blood's fat values.
4. Insulin increases the liver's production of fat substances and causes the fat to lie and slosh around in the arteries for a much longer time. You can't eat many carbohydrates and fats at the same time. One of these substances should be avoided, unless you are a top athlete of course!
5. Eating a lot of carbohydrates (55–60 percent), as the Health Institute recommends, leads to very high level of fat and long-term fat influence, even if you eat as little fat as is recommended (25–30 percent).
6. A possible solution to the dilemma is that all Finns and Norwegians decide to become top athletes. Dietary recommendations are available at all health clinics, and the national nutritional authorities are certainly interested in

assisting. Training advice is available from the Norwegian School of Sport Scienses.

7. However, this is not an especially tempting solution for the Finns and Norwegians who are not particularly used to exercising. In their case, it is probably better to reduce the effect of carbohydrates by eating foods with a low glycemic index and, in addition, to reduce the total carbohydrate content of the diet. Saturated fats can be consumed with pleasure.

8. Saturated fats reduce the fat content in the blood and keep it at an even, low level for a longer time.

9. The solution is probably very simple. Enjoy fats from both the animal and plant world and drop carbohydrates with high GI. Some think that the sale of potatoes and spaghetti should occur in sports stores, for that's where they will reach the appropriate public.

10. If you continue to supply the body with rocket fuel (carbohydrates with high GI) and reduce the r.p.m's with the wrong fats, the motor is bound to develop problems.

11. A health indicator equally informative as the Glycemic Index (GI) is, according to doctoral candidate Tuomasykka, the Lipemic Index (LI). Saturated fat has low LI, and the liquid plant oils have high LI.

12. As an indicator of heart health, it is more important to measure triglycerides in the blood than cholesterol. For the heart and arteries, a high level of triglycerides is more dangerous than high cholesterol.

13. Cholesterol is measured because the pharmaceutical industry has a product (statins) that they want to sell to reduce cholesterol.

14. To lower triglycerides, we don't have to open a bottle of pills. It is enough to start exercising with top athletes or consume fewer carbohydrates.

15. There is a clear connection between triglycerides in the blood and obesity.

16. One possibility for stopping the epidemic of obesity is to drop all snacks between meals and eat only breakfast, lunch, and dinner. Such a regime will make the nutritional industry and grocery stores shed crocodile tears! Nonetheless, it might be more important for the health of the population that people lose weight. Now we are making ourselves fat with these unnecessary meals.

17. It is important to distribute the fat intake throughout our waking hours. It is not sensible to stuff an entire day's fat ration into breakfast. Save a little fat for lunch and dinner too.

18. Humans are created to utilise both fats and carbohydrates. If we eat too little fat and too many carbohydrates an imbalance develops in the body."

Christer Sundqvist, biologist

My comments:

What the Finnish biologist writes is naturally obvious to those of us who eat according to THE SCANDINAVIAN DIET. Nevertheless, it is essential that this old knowledge is repeatedly reiterated, and that debate is opened among the nutritional theologists. Reality is rapidly gaining ground – at least in Finland!

What is now needed is for an economically independent scientist to perform an indisputable, well-documented study of a fat-rich animal diet. The problem is that it will cost many millions of pounds to do this. Such a study wouldn't be accepted in the scientific literature today, but it quite possibly could be awarded a Nobel Prize in twenty to thirty years.

Christer Enkvist, physician in Trollhättan

Dr. Christer Enkvist is a tough critic of the Western world's illness-causing dietary recommendations. He has authored many well-articulated articles on the subject, and I cite from one of them:

"Fat is not dangerous. Obesity has exploded since nutritional specialists have been advising us to avoid fat. But we don't get fat or sick from fat. Do the opposite of what the nutritional specialists say and rather avoid sugar, bread, pasta, rice, and potatoes.

Recently, Scandinavian newspapers have been publishing various nutritional experts' advice on what we should do to avoid gaining weight: eat less fat and exercise more.

The problem is that, during all the decades that nutrition experts have given this advice, obesity has increased exponentially. People, for the most part, have followed this advice, and fat consumption has decreased over the last 20–30 years.

Even so, more and more people grow fatter and fatter. And still the nutrition experts don't consider the possibility that their advice might be wrong. In fact, they continue to provide the same advice year after year. For this reason, it can be said that their advice is one of the causes of obesity …

In the 1950's and 1960's we never cut the fat off the ham, we always drank full fat milk, and fat people were almost non-existent. Once, everyone knew that if you wanted to make pigs fat, you gave them lots of potatoes and grain, that is, carbohydrates. Now, when we want pigs to be lean, we give them soybeans, canola, and whey, that is, proteins and fat …

As early as 1826, the Frenchman Brillat-Savarin wrote in the cookbook classic *The Physiology of Taste* that "corpulence is caused by a diet with far too much flour and starch", and that plant eaters become fat if you feed them potatoes, grain, or flour, but meat eaters never become fat.

In 1854, Professor Ebstein from Göttingen recommended that a diet for obese people that is "particularly effective in reducing the body's softer parts", included a "reduction of carbohydrates, potatoes, sugar, and sweets of all kinds are completely forbidden. One can eat all kinds of meat, and fat in all forms, such as fatty pork and lamb roasts, fatty ham and, if there is no other fat, one should add bone marrow to the soup.»

In other words, do the opposite of what our modern day nutritional specialists' advice. Eat until you are satisfied three times a day, avoid snacks between meals and don't be afraid of fat. You can't get fat or sick from fat.

If you want to lose weight, cut down on or avoid sugar, bread, pasta, rice, and potatoes."

Dr Christer Enkvist

Stop tampering with our food!

Jenny Reimers, a senior physician at Hernösand in Northern Sweden, is one of the many passionate individuals participating in the battle for a natural diet. She writes the following:

"Look at how difficult – some would perhaps also say complicated – it is today to choose the right food!

However, if we hadn't manipulated the materials in factories so they could be stored over long periods of time before being sold, if we hadn't raised all our domesticated animals in the cheapest manner, if we hadn't emptied the sea of fish and krill to make capsules and fish oil powder, if we hadn't intensively cultivated wheat, soybeans, palm oils, maize, and canola to replace raw materials from naturally wild and naturally raised animals, if we hadn't sold kilo upon kilo of shelled nuts so that we could easily eat enormous amounts of linoleic acid ...

If we hadn't done all this, but had instead practised local agriculture on a smaller scale and coastal fishing on a small scale that sold fresh fish – then we would have access to good and healthy raw materials without needing to know anything more about the food's content or function, and still we would be getting sufficient amounts of good food to eat. This is evolution in a nutshell."

Dr Jenny Reimers

Göran Petersson – a wise professor

The escalating epidemic of obesity is attracting increasing scrutiny. While our traditional health authorities are silent, brave doctors, biologists, and biochemists are reacting. In telling the truth they run the risk of making trouble for themselves.

Göran Petersson, Professor in Chemical Environmental Science at Chalmers Technical High School in Gothenburg, is just such a stouthearted person. For over twenty years he has called attention to the poisons that our food contains.

"Our greatest exposure to complex chemical substances is from the food we eat," says Göran Petersson. "In the course of one life, we are subjected to over 20 ton of chemical substances in our food. Most of the contents of today's junk food are environmental poisons that are devastating for humans."

Göran Petersson on sucralose

"Sucralose is an artificial chlorocarbon substance that has been introduced as a sweetener in some brands of ketchup and yoghurt," writes Göran Petersson in an open letter from November 2005. "This flies in the face of the work that environmental organisations, authorities, and municipalities have done for several decades to end the use of chlorocarbon substances."

Göran Petersson on sugar

"Our sugar consumption has increased a hundredfold in our food in only two hundred years. It should come as no surprise that we now see dramatic health consequences in the form of 'metabolic syndromes' like obesity, diabetes, and cardiovascular diseases. These are very real threats to western civilization."

Göran Petersson is not afraid of saturated fat; however, he does warn against the allegedly advantageous fat Flora: "We should avoid over-consumption of polyunsaturated omega-6-fatty acids from seed oils," says the professor. "There are a high number of these fatty acids in the table margarine Flora, the very margarine that is supposed to be so good for your health."

Göran Petersson is highly sceptical of foods like fizzy drinks, concentrated juice, and ice cream: "A fizzy drink makes your blood sugar rise quickly and therefore also your blood's insulin level," the professor points out. "When blood sugar levels drop after an hour or two, a new hunger for sweets develops. Continual blood sugar highs lead eventually to insulin resistance with permanently high insulin levels.

A high insulin level increases both the transformation of sugar to fat and fat storage in fat cells."

Göran Petersson on ice cream

"Sugar in combination with fat makes us more prone to fat formation. The sugar increases the blood's content of the hormone insulin, which channels fat to the fat cells and keeps it there. Ice cream contains about 20 percent sugar and less than half as much fat and is, therefore, extremely conducive to fat formation. Ice cream is often consumed as a refreshing snack between meals. Insulin levels are consequently higher and fat storage more effective than when ice cream is consumed after a good meal."

For me, it is wonderful to read a professor who is completely aware of how hormonally driven weight increase operates.

Yet another quote: "Insulin-driven fat formation is very powerful. Research on animals showed very early that sugar plus fat causes an increase in body fat, even if the body weight remains unchanged. The anti-oxidant defence, and thus the protection against cardiovascular disease, is weakened."

Göran Petersson does the job that the nutritional authorities should be doing. He is a professor in chemistry and can therefore speak freely.

But what would happen to a physician who made similar assertions?

A doctor who won't be silenced

I started this discussion with Dr Calle Carlsson, a well-known free thinker who always states the truth, and who is always uncomfortably direct with the establishment. I will now conclude with another outspoken person, Uffe Ravnskov, doctor of medicine and independent researcher at Lund in southern Sweden.

Uffe Ravnskov has a sharp mind and a keen perspective. He could have had a brilliant academic career if he had learned to remain silent. But he has the "unhealthy" habit of pointing out discrepancies and pulling no punches. You can't do this in a small country like Sweden. His writings are often refused in Sweden, bu are just as often published in international scientific publications.

On 24 April 2007, Uffe Ravnskov received long overdue recognition. He was awarded the prestigious Leo Prize for his tireless research and educational efforts related to saturated fat not increasing the risk of cardiovascular disease, as well as for his well-grounded critique of the cholesterol myth. In connection with the award ceremony, an international seminar on diabetes, fat, and cholesterol was held.

Uffe's articles are often long and full of scientific references. I could have filled this book with such texts. Instead, some quotes from his list of cholesterol facts and a short, popular debate post will have to suffice. If you are interested in learning more about Uffe Ravnskov, you can visit his website at www.ravnskov.nu/cholesterol.htm or visit www.thincs.org.

Cholesterol facts

1. Cholesterol is not a deadly poison, but a substance that is critical for the formation and functioning of all cells. Cholesterol is neither "good" nor "bad". However, the content in the blood is influenced by a number of factors, for example, stress, physical activity, changes in body weight, and smoking.

2. High cholesterol is claimed to be responsible for hardening of the arteries and heart attacks. However, numerous studies show that people with low cholesterol suffer from hardening of the arteries just as often as those with high cholesterol.

3. Our bodies produce 3–4 times more cholesterol than we eat. Production increases when we eat too little cholesterol, and decreases when our food is rich in cholesterol. This explains why it is so difficult to influence cholesterol levels by changing diet.

4. The cholesterol content of food and animal fat have no relationship with the hardening of the arteries or heart attack. For example, over thirty scientific studies show that the amount of fat heart patients ate before they be-

came ill was no greater than the amount eaten by healthy people.

5. Decreasing cholesterol, by using medicines that were available before statins were introduced, can't affect the risk of heart attack death. They are damaging to your health and can shorten your life.

6. The new type of cholesterol-lowering medicines, statins, prevent heart attack, but the effect is very weak and has little to do with lowering cholesterol. Unfortunately, they can cause cancer, at least in test animals. Whether this is also true for humans is impossible to say with certainty, because we have only used statins for ten years. For example, lung cancer due to smoking doesn't appear until long after ten years of smoking.

7. High cholesterol is a risk factor for less than ten percent of those who die from heart attacks. Besides, cholesterol protects against infections. Older people with high cholesterol live longer than older people with low cholesterol.

8. Many of these facts have been presented in scientific journals over the last decades, but few are aware of this research.

9. The reason that laymen, doctors, and most researchers are not aware of these facts, is that all of the results that contradict the message of the cholesterol campaign are ignored or wrongly cited in scientific literature.

Uffe Ravnskov on dietary recommendations

"What is bizarre about the nutritional experts is their demand that dietary recommendations be based on science and practical experience. This is bizarre for the reason that, if you read the scientific articles that the nutritional authorities refer to, including the World Health Organisation's recommendations, you find only two arguments for avoiding saturated fat, and none of them survives close scrutiny.

One argument is that saturated fat causes cholesterol to rise. First of all, this is an argument that, in science, is called indirect evidence – and, secondly, it isn't even correct. Many experiments that have been performed over the last few years show that, even if you cover 20–50 percent of your energy needs with saturated fats, your cholesterol remains stable.

WHO's second argument refers to a study performed by the Willett group at Harvard, where for years they have analysed the diet and heart fatalities of over 80 000 female nurses. WHO maintains that the nurses who ate the most saturated fat also had the highest risk of heart attack. Those who have read the Willett group's study thoroughly know, however, that, after diverse complicating factors were corrected for, the connection was no longer clear. In addition, there are more than twenty comparable studies that fail to show any connection, among them the extensive Malmö study.

A second serious assertion against the present dietary recommendations is that not a single clinical study has shown that a low-fat diet is advantageous, not for diabetics or others. The only experiment that has been performed is the extensive Women's Health Trial, where 20 000 women reduced their fat consumption while 30 000 continued to eat as before. After eight years, the number of heart attacks and the number of deceased were the same in both groups.

Probably the most disturbing advice diabetics receive is to eat more carbohydrates, despite the fact that the main problem for diabetics, as we know, is their problem of processing glucose. I have written more about this in the Swedish journal, *Medicinsk Access*. Today, there are over 25 clinical studies that indicate that a low-carbohydrate diet has considerably better effect on adult-onset diabetes. Four of the studies have lasted six months or more and have had the same positive results as short-term tests."

Uffe Ravnskov, MD and author of *The Great Cholesterol Myths*

Calories, calories, and calories ...

There are two methods for losing weight: energy driven weight loss or hormone-driven weight loss as presented in THE SCANDINAVIAN DIET.

Energy driven weight loss involves reducing your intake of calories and/or increasing your level of exercise. This method is often, incorrectly, called "dieting". Hormone-driven dieting is based on eating in a manner that stimulates fat metabolism and minimises fat storage. You eat until you are satisfied and let nature take care of the rest.

I discovered the hormonal method by pure chance six years ago and immediately started spreading the word. Those I debated with then claimed that the method would not work. It has. I have lost 10 stone 3 (65 kg). Then they claimed that I would get sick. I have not. On the contrary, I have progressed from illness to having a remarkable indicators of good health. Then they claimed that I would regain my weight. I have not done that either. I have maintained my new weight for several years, and I will keep it like this for the rest of my life.

Today there is a slow grassroots revolution. People who are eating according to hormonal principles are eating until they are satisfied and losing weight. And very few of them are counting calories. They have probably realised that most of the calorie counters are often fatter than most people.

Beautiful calorie theories

Even I think that the calorie theory is a beautiful theory. It would, of course, be fantastic if we could eat according to a calorie table and know ahead of time whether you were going to go up or down in weight. Everything would be so simple! The catch is that the body doesn't count calories.

The Swedish diet professor Stephan Rössner believes strongly in calories. According to him, the only thing that counts is how many calories we ingest and how many calories we use. Yet, when he discusses this theory, he keeps stumbling over examples that prove him wrong!

In the book *"Lose weight" with Stephan Rössner,* he presents a large Canadian study that compares big eaters and light eaters. The big eaters ate twice as much as the light eaters per pound of body weight, but they weighed on average 2 stone (13 kg) less! Both groups exercised just as much. The professor thought these results puzzling, and demands, as usual, more research.

In fact, these results aren't at all surprising. They are simply one of many indications that the calorie theory doesn't work.

Marion Apfelbaum's study from the Warsaw ghetto between 1943 and 1945 illustrates what happens when the calorie theory is really put into practice. The prisoners' caloric requirements were 2500 kcal per day, but they scarcely received a third of that. Instead, they were on starvation rations. How much weight should they have lost? It is easy to calculate based on the calorie theory.

Their caloric deficiency was 1700 kcal per day. If we calculate that each gram of fat tissue corresponds to 7 kcal, their fat loss should have been 240 g per day (240 x 7 = 1700). In other words, they should have lost about 1 stone 2 (7 kg) per month. After 24 months, they should have lost 27 stone 7 lb (175 kg), or in other words, disappeared. In reality, they lost a pound per month, or 2 stone 3 l (14 kg) in two years. Their weight loss was only 8 percent of the calculated value. What happened with the other 92 percent? The calorie theory is unable to explain this.

What the calorie theory doesn't take into account is hormonal effects. When times are lean, the body's starvation response kicks in. If a person starts to overeat, the body's rate of metabolism increases. This mechanism is also hormone-driven.

I have experienced the starvation response myself, sometimes for years, and I remember well the suffering involved in going to bed every night hungry, and even so not losing any weight. Thus the joy was great when I finally discovered that weight is hormone-driven. That's when I could start the enjoyable hobby of eating myself to weight loss.

Four comments on calories

When I started my successful dieting, I ate until I was satisfied on really fatty foods. There was no reason to count calories, for the goal wasn't to lose weight (at the time I too was convinced that you had to count calories to lose weight). I probably consumed somewhere between 3 000 and 6 000 calories a day. However, the decisive factor was not the calorie intake, but that I metabolised what I ate. Yes, I even metabolised some of my stored fat.

Today I can't eat that way. There is only about half of me left, and my stomach has shrunk. But I still eat until I am satisfied, just as I did six years ago.

I am asked how many calories a day one should consume, and I repeat time and time again that the question itself is incorrect. To avoid having to answer this question over and over again I have collected a few of the comments that I have written on this topic. They were written in different situations and with different aims, but I still stand by every word.

The first comment

Hi Sten Sture!

I understand that you question the calorie theory, and that you believe you can increase your caloric intake and still lose weight. But isn't a calorie still a calorie? Don't you believe in the basic principles of thermodynamics?

Answer:

Thank you for your question. What you have hit upon, here, is a general misunderstanding.

I don't question the calorie theory in the sense that different types of fuel emit different amounts of heat when they are burned in an oven. I have, however, asserted that the calorie theory has little value for an overweight person who wants to lose weight. The amount of energy (calories) actually says nothing about how a food product influences our natural system of weight regulation.

Notice that I refer to natural weight regulation, what occurs in open biological systems, for example in mammals. This weight regulation is hormone-driven and is primarily influenced by what we eat, and by the hormonal responses of the body. To put it simply: if we eat to achieve fat storage, we will store extra fat, even on an average energy intake. If we eat to achieve fat metabolism, we will burn surplus fat even with a relatively high energy intake.

I have no reason to question the laws of thermodynamics; they certainly apply to closed systems. But human beings are an open system, and we do much more with food than simply transform it to heat.

I don't claim that we can eat more than we metabolise and still lose weight. That would be a ridiculous claim. What I say is that the question is incorrectly formulated. We can't take the position that metabolism is a constant, and that the only way to influence body weight is to decrease fuel intake or to increase exercise. (Yes, there are energy-driven diet programs too, but they usually don't succeed because people don't like to be hungry.)

What I do is to turn this reasoning on its head. I say that if we metabolise what we eat, then we can't increase our weight, no matter how much we eat. If, on the other hand, we don't metabolise what we eat, then we can get fat on next to nothing. It was this insight that made it possible for me to develop my program for hormone driven weight loss.

I hope that this helps you understand THE SCANDINAVIAN DIET.

Sten Sture Skaldeman

Another comment:

Can we consume unlimited calories when we eat a fat-rich diet? I don't think so. But the flexibility we have varies from person to person. People who easily maintain their weight can consume considerable amounts of fat without gaining a gram. They simply turn their metabolism up a notch. Really overweight people can also eat large portions of fat, but they must usually reduce their calorie consumption.

In my view, calories are an uninteresting "pseudo" measurement for human food consumption. They say nothing about what our bodies do with food. On the other hand, calories are a useful measurement when we want to know how food functions as fuel in an oven.

The decisive factor is whether you burn what you eat, or whether you store it as fat. This has much more to do with the composition of the food than with the energy content. Eat a lot of fat and few carbohydrates, and most of us can eat much more than if the distribution was the other way around. This applies especially to insulin resistant people.

What does this mean in practice? Well, it means that people have to learn to recognise the body's hunger signals and provide it with the food it needs. A fatty low carbohydrate diet means that some people consume more calories than before, while others consume less.

I measured my own energy intake for many months during the period that I tested my diet program. I consumed on average 600–700 calories more per day when I maintained my very fat-rich diet. On this diet I rapidly lost weight. Then I increased the side dishes, lowered the energy intake, and the weight loss slowed down.

Today, I rarely count calories, but when I do, I eat about 2000 kcal per day. Sometimes I eat 3000, other times 1500. During the course of my weight loss period, I often ate substantially more, but I was also much larger.

My conclusion, after some years of correspondence with different dieters, is that those who are very overweight have a greater degree of flexibility, while those who are closer to their normal weight must hold a careful eye on every parameter, including calories. Our body simply doesn't like to lose as much weight as we would like it to given modern ideals of beauty.

One of the world's most competent diet doctors is Blake F. Donaldson. He has helped tens of thousands of extremely overweight patients lose weight. Donaldson puts it like this: "It is possible that an upper limit exists for how much you can eat on a fat and entirely animal diet, but I have yet to discover where that limit goes."

However, you should be aware that most of Donaldson's patients were enormous. He might express himself differently if he had treated people with normal weight. Or maybe he wouldn't!

Sten Sture

A third comment on the same topic

Disregard the calories, but don't eat more than you need! That is how you can sum up my position on the eternal question of calories.

The question of whether we can consume unlimited calories is a question for a calorie counter. Can we eat unlimited amounts of green things? Or of yellow things? If yellow consists of some kind of oil, maybe yes; if it consists of cake, we cannot. For me personally, it is difficult to overeat on a fatty animal diet. If I eat 1 200 calories at breakfast, I can often wait until evening before I eat again.

You should eat when your body is hungry. Then you should provide your body with what it needs. If you eat when the body isn't hungry, most people (but not all) will gain weight. It is difficult to gain weight on fat. This was clearly shown a generation ago when the calorie theory was disproved. But such studies had to stop when the alleged dangers of fat became dogma.

Someone with access to a medical library should scan in all the old studies and put them online. The only one that I have seen online is a study where the fat intake was increased systematically to see what would happen. This study was performed in the early 1970's and is called *Response of body weight to a low carbohydrate, high fat diet in normal and obese subjects* (H. Kasper, H. Thiel, and M. Ehl).

"In normal subjects, the fat content of a formula diet in the form of corn oil and olive oil (but with constant carbohydrate and protein intake) was raised continually up to a daily ingestion of more than 6 800 fat calories. Under normal utilisation of fat in the gastrointestinal tract, it was seen that there was only a slight weight gain, compared with the caloric intake. This effect was particularly conspicuous with corn oil and less so with olive oil. The two oils differ by their linoleic acid content."

Notice that the insignificant weight gain occurs with unchanged carbohydrate intake. With a diet significantly lower in carbohydrates, there would probably have been no weight gain at all.

Researcher Dashti from Kuwait has recently taken up this approach. He puts people on low carbohydrate diets with a large portion of olive oil. Beyond that, the test individuals may eat as much as they want. They go drastically down in weight and recover from their diabetes.

It would appear that Dashti is not aware that he is operating in a forbidden area. He is presumably doing research with state support. If he continues to follow this direction, he will sooner or later meet fierce opposition.

Too bad he can't find out what unlimited meat consumption does for a person!

Sten Sture

A fourth comment:

If we eat more than we metabolise, we get fat. This is self-explanatory. But that doesn't mean that we have to eat less to lose weight! We don't need to exercise more either, even though exercise has real value.

A human's metabolism is not analogous to combustion in a steam engine. Humans are an open system, and we follow other rules. If we reduce our food intake, we may lose weight, but we get a machine that doesn't function as well; a machine that produces less useful products, and that doesn't doesn't optimally.

From studies of reality we know that caloric limitation seldom works on a long-term basis. Daily, hundreds of millions of people follow these different steam engine theories. They eat less and go to bed hungry, but in principle they all stay fat. Even so, the professors draw no conclusions from the fiasco.

In an emergency, we can, of course, starve ourselves to weight loss, but it is a temporary solution. The weight we lose returns when we stop starving ourselves.

What the professors don't know – or don't want to know – is that storage and fat metabolism are hormone-driven. By eating to achieve fat metabolism, we can lose weight without removing a single calorie from our diet and without doing a single minute of exercise.

This doesn't mean that everyone can eat without limitations, but it does mean that those who eat to achieve fat metabolism can eat more than those who eat sparingly.

Millions of people have managed to eat their way to weight loss since the days of William Banting. In Sweden, dieting is even called *"banting"*. Despite the fact that there is an overwhelming amount of evidence, almost no research has been done in this area. The explanation is that there is no pharmaceutical firm or junk food producer who is willing to finance such research. If people ate their way to health and weight loss on natural foods, it would be a catastrophe for those who finance the research. And likewise it would be a catastrophe for all the professors who make their living claiming that humans work like steam engines.

Sten Sture Skaldeman

Why am I
not losing weight?

Once you have read this far, you have hopefully received a good start on your journey to health. I assume that you have come through the first difficult week, and that you have gradually started to feel more energetic and healthy and strong. This is an improvement that will increase in the coming months.

If you belong to the majority, you have already achieved some weight loss. About three out of four do. My female standard students lose an average of 2 stone 5 (15 kg) per year, while their husbands lose twice that. A few women have metabolised over 6 stone 4 (40 kg) of fat in a single year, but in my opinion that is not necessarily a favourable result. You should be kind to your body, and avoid violent changes. Your health is of primary importance!

Some continue to burn fat at a good rate, but add the same weight in the form of muscle. In that case you have to use clothes or a measuring tape to control your progress. The only thing these people need to do to be satisfied is throw out their bathroom scales!

One out of four or five people have trouble increasing their metabolism of fat. For many of these people it is not the diet, but other factors that are just as important. When I advise such a person, we usually find a solution. Let me summarise the most common reasons for a lack of desired weight loss.

The five most common explanations for not losing weight:

1. *Your body is uncertain about what is happening*

This is the most common explanation. And yet, you never read about it in regular diet books. Are you in the habit of starving your body from time to time? If so, your body is uncertain about what is happening and has responded by saving its fat. Do you switch back and forth between different diet programs? In this case, too, your body is confused. The solution is to establish stable habits and convince your body that enough food is available – the right kind of food!

2. *You eat too little fat*

A high amount of fat in the diet induces the body to burn fat. Low fat food does the opposite. The more fat that you eat, the more fat you burn. If you are very overweight, at least 70 percent of your daily energy intake should come from fat. In my experience, saturated fats are best, and polyunsaturated fats are worst. (If you hover around a normal weight, a protein-rich diet may be an alternative).

3. *You eat too many carbohydrates*

Carbohydrates cause blood sugar to rise, resulting in the release of more insulin. Insulin blocks fat metabolism. Therefore, you don't lose weight. It is especially bad if you eat carbohydrates and fat at the same time. Hidden amounts of carbohydrates exist in almost all commercially produced food. Avoid all manufactured food!

4. *You don't sleep well*

Becoming new and healthy again is challenging for your body. You need proper nutrition and rest to complete the project. An exhausted body saves its reserves. Try to get fresh air and sunshine every day. That is the best solution for all sorts of insomnia.

5. *You eat something that hinders your weight loss*

A common mistake is to eat fruit as a snack between meals. This stops weight loss for most people. Cheese, nuts, or coffee can prevent weight loss for some. I don't lose weight when I eat nuts, but I can eat as much cheese as I want. We are all different.

PS. If you use anti-depressive medications or insulin, you can gain lots of weight very quickly. I have observed many such cases among my students. THE SCANDINAVIAN DIET stabilises blood sugar and dampens mood swings. It is very possible that GI-Zero! will permit you to become medicine-free.

Good luck! Again: look at the publisher's web page, – www.littlemoonpublishing.com – as well as www.thescandinaviandiet.co.uk –

there you will find useful links, references, interviews, and reports.

Register

Lose Your Excess Fat ... Get Your Optimal Health!
Without Ever Having To Feel Hungry Again!

Go to our web page www.scandinaviandiet.co.uk
or ring 01614082979 for more information and
allow me to help you!

Warmly,

Victoria Aase
Licensed Scandinavian Diet Coach